The Beginning Reading Handbook

Strategies for Success

GAIL HEALD-TAYLOR

HEINEMANN
Portsmouth, NH

This book is dedicated to my grandchildren
Nathan, Matthew, Amy, Kasey, and Kody

Heinemann
A division of Reed Elsevier Inc.
361 Hanover Street
Portsmouth, NH 03801–3912
www.heinemann.com

Offices and agents throughout the world

The author and publisher wish to thank those who have generously given permission to reprint borrowed material:

Excerpts from *The Chick and The Duckling* by Mirra Ginsburg are reprinted with the permission of Simon & Schuster Books for Young Readers, an imprint of Simon & Schuster Children's Publishing Division. Text Copyright © 1972 by Mirra Ginsburg.

Library of Congress Cataloging-in-Publication Data

Heald-Taylor, Gail.
    The beginning reading handbook : strategies for success / Gail Heald-Taylor.
      p. cm.
    Includes bibliographical references.
    ISBN 0-325-00333-5 (alk. paper)
    1. Reading (Early childhood)—Handbooks, manuals, etc.   2. Children—Books and reading—Handbooks, manuals, etc.   I. Title.

    LB1139.5.R43 H43 2001
    372.4—dc21

2001039009

Editor: Lois Bridges
Production service: Patricia Adams
Production coordination: Abigail M. Heim
Cover design: Kathy Squires
Cover photo: Lisa Fowler
Manufacturing: Steve Bernier

Printed in the United States of America on acid-free paper
05 04 03 02 01 RRD 1 2 3 4 5

Contents

. . . .

Acknowledgments

· ·

The children I have worked with over the years have taught me much about how young children learn; however, it is my grandchildren who have reminded me of the joy of the literacy journey. They have shown me that all the strategies in this book really work. I especially want to thank Nathan, Matthew, Amy, Kasey, and Kody who love the books I send them and the stories we create together.

I am grateful to the many teachers I have worked with over the years who had the courage to implement the many strategies in this book. In particular, I would like to acknowledge several teachers in Waterloo County, Ontario who believed in me and the literacy strategies we implemented together so many years ago. Shelley Kropf and Cathy Van der Horst were the first to implement dictated stories with their first graders and taught me what could be learned from this process. Wayne Gingrich showed me how to use literature in creative ways to entice his learning disabled students to read and write. Wendy Brum shared how first graders could interpret literature in their Big Books through water color and collage. As well, Laura Hedges' kindergarten class in J. C. Parks School, Indian Head, Maryland demonstrated how young children think at high levels as they use literature across the curriculum. I have used Big Books from their classrooms in seminars I have conducted across North America and Southeast Asia.

Samples of children's work helped to make the various strategies in this book come alive. Therefore, I am grateful to these teachers for sharing their treasures: Victoria Bazeley, Ron Brown, Wendy Brum, Cathy Franklin, Wayne Gingrich, Laura Hedges, Jeanette Moore, and Geraldine Van de Kleut.

Geraldine Van de Kleut, Cathy Franklin, and Ron Brown also gave me valuable advice and suggestions for improving the book. They always enrich my vision of literacy.

I particularly want to thank Lois Bridges, my editor, for her constant encouragement, guidance, and enthusiasm for the book. Through our daily communication we have become good friends. I also thank Patty Adams, the production editor for this book, for her attention to detail and suggestions for changes in order to communicate my ideas more clearly.

I appreciate Kristi Setterington for taking many of the photographs for this book. Her wonderful, relaxed manner with the children produced so many candid shots.

I especially thank Arleen Downs, my lifelong friend, who has always been there for me in all my educational endeavors.

Finally, I want to thank my husband John for his endless encouragement, sense of humor, and love. I particularly appreciated the periodic breaks he encouraged me to take from writing to go out for lunch and his reminders to watch the swans out on the lake.

Introduction

· ·

This book for early school years educators is a practical guide for developing literacy in children between the ages of three to seven. Although many aspects of literacy are addressed, such as reading, speaking, listening, and writing, the predominant focus is on reading. This is not a book about theory, although theoretical aspects and current research are sometimes discussed, but rather, this handbook contains numerous specific strategies for teachers that are easily implemented with young children to make learning to read a truly joyous experience. At the same time, these activities will build the foundation of literacy that leads to long-term success in school.

A further feature of this handbook is the support it provides teachers in extending learning with parents at home. Small articles and letters to parents designated by the

symbol are provided on the Heinemann website at <http://www.heinemann.com/heald-taylor/> and teachers who purchase this book are welcome to download and send them home to parents in order to build their understanding about the strategies used in the classroom.

Numerous topics important in developing literacy are incorporated into this handbook. In Chapter One I discuss the nature of early years children regarding their physical, emotional, and intellectual development. I also talk about the developmental aspects of learning to read. I do this to emphasize that learning to read is a gradual process spanning several years from birth to age seven and beyond. Also important is the fact that no two children develop in the same way nor at the same speed, and I discuss ways to deal with this natural phenomenon. Four reading phases are outlined to help teachers observe the natural development of their students. I call them the Emergent, Beginning, Developing, and Independent phases of reading. An easy-to-administer informal reading test is also available to assist teachers in determining the developmental phase in which their children are associated.

Chapter Two is devoted to describing ways to organize the classroom and how to set up learning centers. Specific, practical ready-to-use learning activities related to listening, speaking, reading, writing, art, and drama are detailed. Various types of literature such as predictable pattern literature, wordless books, and informational books are described and ways to obtain literature selections are also discussed.

Chapter Three outlines instructional strategies supporting Emergent and Beginning readers. These include several read-aloud strategies for books without words, predictable pattern literature, refrain books, complex picture books, and issue books. Other strategies that support early literacy are also described such as dictated stories, dictated sentences, chart stories, shared reading, and making Big Books. I also address ways to develop sentence, word, and phonic understandings.

Chapter Four describes strategies for Developing and Independent readers. These strategies focus on developing recognition of sentences, phrases, and words. Several strategies to build understanding of letters and phonics within meaningful contexts are also explained. Guided reading procedures are also outlined in this chapter to provide early readers with the necessary support leading to independence. As well, ways to implement individualized reading are discussed.

Chapter Five deals with ways to use informational books and ways to organize thematic units and author studies.

Assessing student progress and communicating with parents is the focus of Chapter Six. Here I talk about varieties of ways of collecting information regarding student growth such as anecdotal records, learning logs, samples of work, reading conferences, learning journals, portfolios, and self-evaluation. Standardized testing is also discussed in this chapter. In addition, various ways to communicate with parents are outlined.

Finally, Appendix D contains numerous literature selections to assist teachers in planning for reading aloud, shared reading, sentence, word, and phonic study. As well, lists of informational books, selections for themes interesting to young children, and selections by particular authors young children enjoy are also provided. (A complete bibliography of all titles categorized in Appendix D, organized alphabetically, is available on the Heinemann website at <http://www.heinemann.com/heald-taylor/>.)

Building the Foundation for Literacy

To effectively develop literacy in young children, several basic understandings need to be considered. First, we need to understand the nature of early primary-aged children regarding their physical, emotional, and intellectual needs. We also need to understand the developmental learning phases generally associated with Beginning readers to plan appropriate literacy programs for them. Also important in planning for literacy is an understanding of the main teacher-led approaches to learning to read. These approaches are outlined in this chapter.

THE NATURE OF YOUNG CHILDREN

Early years children, between the ages of three and six, are generally joyful, active, enthusiastic, and love everything new, exciting, and adventurous.

At the same time they can be impulsive, egocentric, and dependent. They count on teachers and caregivers for almost everything: finding a note from their parent, comforting them when they fall down, putting band-aids on scuffed knees, and finding a sweater they misplaced. Responsive, caring adults who can tie literacy programs into caregiving are a must for young children because the literary experiences in the early years are the foundation of learning for the rest of their school career. Following are characteristics of physical, emotional, and intellectual development typical of early years children.

Physical Development

Children in the early years are in constant motion. They wiggle, fall out of chairs, run around and chase each other, and climb on everything. Because their muscles grow fast and uneven, they often lose balance and fall over playground equipment, balls, and toys. They also may have difficulty hopping, skipping, and catching. Nevertheless, large muscles are more highly developed than fine muscles in their wrists and fingers. In order for them to continue to develop physically, consider the following:

• **Activity:** Young children thrive on activity; they love singing, action songs, and games that help them release energy and gain both large and fine muscle control.

• **Breaks:** Children in the early years need many opportunities to move around and engage in numerous physical activities and games. They are able to sit still at tables or on the floor for no more than fifteen-minute intervals.

• **Handwriting:** Many early primary children are unable to effectively grip pencils and paint brushes because the development of bones and muscles in wrists and fingers develop later than the rest of their body. Consequently, they may have difficulty printing on lines, forming letters, coloring, and drawing. This is especially problematic for boys, since girls' physical development may be six to twelve months ahead of boys'. Therefore, instead of formal handwriting exercises, fine motor dexterity is best developed by modeling with play dough, clay, or plasticine and constructing with blocks.

Eye Development   Since the eyes of young children are not fully mature, too much close work could injure their nervous systems and cause muscular disorders. Thus, too many activities involving worksheets may be harmful to young children. The same restraint should be considered with computer activities.

Hearing   Hearing is also not fully developed in many youngsters, which may cause them difficulty in distinguishing between sounds of letters.

Coordination   Coordination of eyes, hearing, and grasping is still developing during these early years, making it difficult to distinguish sound/symbol relationships and also interfering with their ability to copy from blackboards and charts.

Rest and Relaxation   Although many young children have high energy, they tire easily and therefore may have difficulty completing tasks. Therefore, a rest time should be incorporated into the day, whether it be a nap or quiet story time.

Emotional Development

Early years children are generally egocentric and more concerned with their own needs than those of others. They are often independent, self-controlled, self-confident, and eager to have responsibility, and at other times they become boastful, self-assertive, impulsive, and volatile. In order to support emotional growth, be mindful of the following:

• Offer encouragement: Children in the early years need lots of praise, warmth, and approval.

• Provide security: They need to feel secure and cared about with adults who are patient, kind, and responsive to their needs.

• Foster friendships: All youngsters thrive emotionally when they have many social interactions with their peers in class and on the playground.

• Establish routines: Most children function best in predictable environments where there is structure, supervision, and guidance.

Intellectual Development

Children's intellectual development makes great strides during the early years, especially in the areas of listening, speaking, reading, and writing.

Listening   By the time children are five, many have a listening vocabulary of over 20,000 words. They are able to listen to others, receive new ideas, and listen to directions. They can gain information from hearing books read to them and enjoy many forms of writing such as rhymes, poetry, pattern books, picture books, and informational material.

Speaking   Children's speaking ability develops rapidly during the early years. They use language to inform, imagine, reason, and predict. Further, they can tell stories with suspense and expression. However, their ideas are frequently expressed in loosely connected sentences, and they often confuse many grammar conventions such as plurals and tenses.

Reading   Reading ability grows dramatically during the preschool and early primary years. At first, children show an interest in books and want books read to them. Soon they begin to model adult reading as they pretend to read books themselves, relying on pictures, meaning, and memory to guide their "reading." As they listen to, look at, and read books for themselves, they develop many skills about print such as holding books right side up, turning pages, and pointing to words. They also learn many words in familiar print material such as predictable pattern stories, poetry, charts, sentence strips, and dictated stories. Many children begin to read a variety of printed material (predictable stories, poetry, and dictated stories) and use several cueing strategies; semantics (meaning), syntax (structure), graphophonics (letter/sound) sometime during the early primary grades.

Writing   During the early years children communicate their thoughts mainly through speaking, storytelling, and dictating stories. However, many start to communicate through their drawings, scribbles, and writing. Although you may not be able to read their writing, they frequently

intend their invented marks to communicate messages and may ask you to read their scribble ("What does this say, Dad?")

Supporting Language Development   In order to support children's abilities in language development, early childhood educators should keep the following in mind:

Listening   Young children gain listening ability through many oral interactions with their peers during center activities. They also develop listening skills during read-aloud sessions and when they listen to books on audiotapes at listening centers.

Speaking   Like listening, speaking ability matures during interactions with peers in various learning centers. Speaking ability also develops significantly when children dictate stories regularly. Good models of effective language are found in the variety of literature that is read to them. Circle time and sharing activities also foster confidence in speaking.

Reading   Reading develops rapidly during the early years, especially when children participate in a number of specific activities designed to promote reading.

Early Reading Strategies

Children become aware of the function of print when early years teachers guide them in read-aloud sessions, the shared reading process, the dictation of personal stories, sentence strip exercises, and guided reading activities. All these activities are outlined in this book.

Writing   The foundation for independent writing begins in the early years. Children can be successful composing stories by orally dictating while an adult records their words. Children's own personal writing also makes positive strides in the early primary years, especially when teachers accept their approximate spellings and celebrate when spellings gradually become standard.

Informing Parents About the Nature of Young Children

In order to help parents understand the nature of young children, we encourage you to copy Parent Letter 1 and send it home with the children.

DEVELOPMENTAL PHASES OF READING

As early years educators, we are keenly aware that children of the same age develop in different ways and at different rates. Nevertheless, we also know that patterns of growth follow a range of predictable developmental benchmarks. For example, we expect that babies will smile, roll over, cut their first teeth, stand up unassisted, and speak sometime between the age of three months to three years, but any individual baby is unlikely to demonstrate a particular behavior at precisely the same time as another of the same age. We also know that overall development of young children is generally predictable. For instance, before three years they will likely be able to walk, have a full a set of teeth, and speak in phrases and sentences.

Similarly, in learning to read there are benchmarks of growth that can be predicted, even though some children reach these milestones more quickly than others. Children develop in their own ways and cannot be rushed before they are ready. Just as a child cannot be forced to walk prematurely, it would be a mistake to force a child to read, write, or spell perfectly until they have reached certain benchmarks of literacy.

DEVELOPMENTAL PHASES OF READING DEVELOPMENT

Learning to read usually spans several years, since some children begin to read during their preschool years, while others do not begin to read until they reach the age of seven (second grade). Thus, one cannot predict a certain set of reading behaviors for any precise age or grade. However, most children do develop literacy through the following predictable phases, even though some will develop faster or slower than others.

Following is a summary of developmental phases that describe reading behaviors of some preschoolers, as well as children in the early primary grades (kindergarten to second grade). Following the description of the developmental phase is a list of strategies that will help children reach the behaviors listed in this phase. A more detailed list of reading behaviors is outlined in the Developmental Reading Behavior Inventory found in Appendix A.

Emergent Reading Phase

In the Emergent phase, children learn much about reading.

Comprehension   Children in this phase become interested in books and enjoy hearing stories read to them. Children learn so much from listening to stories: they learn about characters and their adventures, how stories work, and are introduced to rich vocabulary. Listening to stories also provides opportunities to develop comprehension such as understanding main ideas, details, and concepts in stories. Through listening, children become aware of characters and events and like to demonstrate their understanding through art, drama activities, and role play reading.

Concepts of Books   Children at the Emergent phase learn many concepts about print materials. They understand that books have authors and illustrators and they become familiar with certain authors. They also learn that print material is organized in different formats (predictable literature, dictated stories, chart stories, poetry, songs, and Big Books).

Early Reading Behaviors   Children in the Emergent phase employ many early reading behaviors such as looking at books and retelling stories that have been read to them. In fact, their retelling of stories is often so close to the original text that they appear to be actually "reading" even though they do not attend to the print itself. However, at this phase, children also begin to recognize how print works: that text is written in a left to right direction from top to bottom of pages, that pages are turned left to right, and that marks on pages carry messages. During this "experimental" phase children begin to "read" along with adults as they read together the repeated lines and refrains and they begin to retell familiar stories with a great deal of accuracy.

Word Knowledge   Children begin to pay attention to words during this phase as they begin to point to clumps of words and assign oral responses. They also begin to point to words in familiar contexts such as dictated sentence strips, predictable pattern stories, class charts, and Big Books. They begin to ask what certain words say and start to recognize a few of the words in familiar print material in the formats described above. By the end of the Emergent phase, children are able to identify approximately ten different words.

Reading Strategies   Reading strategies employed by children in the Emergent phase are limited to semantics (pictures, memory of stories, personal experiences) and syntax (repeated words, phrases, sentences, and refrains). The graphophonic component is often too abstract for most children in the Emergent phase.

Rate of Learning   Children may be in the Emergent phase sometime between the ages of three to six, while a few children may move through this phase later. This is a natural phenomenon, since young children progress at very different rates.

Developmental Reading Behavior Inventory   See Appendix A, the Developmental Reading Behavior Inventory, for a more comprehensive list of reading behaviors at the Emergent phase.

Literary Experiences to Support Learning in the Emergent Phase

Several reading strategies support reading growth at the Emergent phase.

Comprehension   Children develop an understanding of what is read to them as they participate in numerous read-aloud sessions as outlined in Chapter Three, *Reading Aloud Predictable Pattern Literature to Develop Comprehension, Reading Aloud Refrain Books*, and *Reading Aloud Complex Picture Books*. Listening and comprehension are also promoted when children respond to literature in a variety of ways as outlined in *Activities for Learning Centers* in Chapter Two, in the section *Ways to Respond to Literature* and during the *Shared Reading Process* (Chapter Three).

Concepts of Books   Children learn about books and how they work when teachers make them aware of titles, authors, and illustrators, and how pages are turned during the various read-aloud strategies in Chapter Three. As well, they become aware of print as they observe teachers scribe for chart stories, dictated stories, and sentences. See *Dictating Stories, Dictating Sentences,* and *Chart Stories* in Chapter Three.

Reading Behaviors   Many early reading behaviors such as print awareness are developed during read-aloud activities especially, *Reading Aloud Predictable Literature to Develop Print Awareness*, the *Shared Reading Process, The Dictated Story Process*, and during *The Dictated Sentence Procedure* (Chapter Three).

Word Knowledge   A more direct focus on word knowledge begins during the *Shared Reading Process* and in the *Dictated Sentence Procedure* as outlined in Chapter Three.

Reading Strategies   Children in the Emergent phase mainly employ semantic and syntactic reading strategies during the read-aloud strategies and when they read their dictated sentences. Children are introduced to the phonics strategy during the *Shared Reading Process* (Chapter Three).

Informing Parents About the Emergent Reading Phase

Parent Letter 2 outlines this phase for parents. You may copy it and send it home with the children.

Beginning Reading Phase

Children in the Beginning reading phase continue to demonstrate many of the behaviors identified in the Emergent phase such as listening to stories, predicting events, recalling details, recognizing authors, retelling stories as though they are reading, and identifying print in the environment as well as in familiar reading material (predictable pattern literature, chart stories, Big Books, and dictated stories).

Comprehension   Children in the Beginning phase gain information from listening to stories. They learn to recall events, main ideas, and details. From listening to stories they also hear how stories are structured with characters, events, and endings.

Concepts of Books   During the Beginning phase children learn many concepts about printed material including the roles of authors and illustrators. They also begin to recognize works from familiar authors and request to have books read to them by authors they like. In addition, they become familiar with different ways print material is organized (predictable, pattern books, picture books, chart stories, poetry, Big Books, and nonfiction).

Reading Behaviors   Reading behaviors develop dramatically during the Beginning phase. Children begin to recall sentence strips, repeated phrases, sentences, and refrains in predictable pattern selections. They also begin to point to individual words in familiar texts and gradually begin to identify a few individual words.

Word Knowledge   Concepts of words develop rapidly in this phase as children begin to match word cards to the same words in sentence strips, read signs and labels around the classroom and school, and read words in familiar material such as pattern books, Big Books, sentence strips, and chart stories. By the end of this phase children will recognize about 30 different words or more.

Reading Strategies   Children in the Beginning phase continue to employ mainly semantic reading strategies (pictures, meaning, memory, and background experiences) to guide their reading. They also employ syntax strategies as they read repeated words, phrases, sentences, and refrains accurately. A few children may begin to employ phonics principles like recognizing initial consonants in familiar materials such as chart stories, sentence strips, and predictable pattern literature.

Oral Reading   By the end of the Beginning phase children are able to read independently about ten familiar sentence strips, about five predictable pattern selections, and recognize approximately 30 individual words. At this phase children read each word on a page slowly and deliberately.

Rate of Learning   Most children reach the Beginning reading phase sometime between kindergarten and second grade.

Developmental Reading Behavior Inventory   A comprehensive list of behaviors associated with the Beginning phase is found in the Developmental Reading Behavior Inventory in Appendix A.

Literacy Activities to Support Learning in the Beginning Phase

Many strategies provide support to children in the Beginning phase.

Comprehension   Listening and comprehension ability continue to strengthen through the various read-aloud strategies outlined in Chapter Three. Comprehension is also promoted when children respond to literature in a variety of ways as outlined in the section, *Learning Activities for Centers* (Chapter Two), *Ways to Respond to Literature,* and during the *Shared Reading Process* in Chapter Three.

Concepts of Books   Concepts of print, awareness of sentences, phrases, and words are reinforced as children dictate stories and sentences and engage in the shared reading process. Children become aware of book concepts when they participate in read-aloud sessions where children are introduced to different print genre (predictable literature, poetry, refrain books, and complex picture books) and a variety of different authors.

Reading Behaviors   Progress in reading such as attending to print, pointing to words, and recognizing sentences occurs during a number of strategies outlined in Chapter Three (various read-aloud procedures, the *Shared Reading Process, The Dictated Story Process,* and during *The Dictated Sentence Procedure*).

Word Knowledge   Word knowledge is developed effectively during the *Shared Reading Process* and the *Dictated Sentence Procedure* where children copy words and match words to sentences.

Reading Strategies   Children in the Beginning phase become more familiar with semantic and syntax reading strategies during the read-aloud strategies, shared reading, and when they read their dictated sentences and stories (Chapter Three). The graphophonic strategy is introduced during the shared reading strategy.

Informing Parents About the Beginning Phase of Reading

In order to inform parents about the Beginning phase of reading, copy and send home Parent Letter 3.

Developing Reading Phase

During the Developing phase children's growth in reading ability accelerates.

Comprehension   During the Developing phase children continue to gain meaning from books that are read to them as they predict events and recall many details, ideas, and concepts in stories they hear. Further, they develop deeper understandings of story structures (characters, events, problems, endings) and notice how stories relate to their own experiences.

Concepts of Books   Children develop many concepts of print material during the Developing phase: they extend their recognition of genre to include pattern books, complex picture books, poetry, chart stories, lists, and nonfiction. They understand the function of authors and illustrators; they continue to recognize more authors by their particular styles and choose series books by particular titles, authors, and genre.

Reading Behaviors   Reading behaviors grow rapidly during this phase. Children move beyond retelling familiar stories to actually reading them. At first their reading is slow and deliberate as they attempt to read each word on the page. But soon they begin to read familiar material with confidence. By the end of the Developing phase, children are able to read independently about ten familiar pattern selections, and about 15 sentence strips.

Word Knowledge   Word knowledge expands during this phase. Children recognize words in many familiar contexts (chart stories, dictated sentences, pattern literature, and Big Books). They also sort known words in a number of different ways and create new sentences from word cards they know. By the end of the Developing phase children recognize about 50 different words.

Reading Strategies   Reading strategies at the Developing phase include graphophonics as well as semantic and syntactic strategies as children begin to identify beginning and ending sounds in familiar words.

Rate of Learning   Children demonstrate behaviors in the Developing phase sometime during the early primary years (first or second grade), since research suggests that learning to read usually occurs anywhere from age five to age seven. Some children simply take a little longer to reach this phase than others.

Developmental Reading Behavior Inventory   A more comprehensive list of behaviors associated with the Developing phase is found in Appendix A in the Developmental Reading Behavior Inventory.

Literary Strategies to Support Learning During the Developing Phase

Several strategies outlined in Chapters Three, Four, and Five also promote reading ability during the Developing phase. These include the following:

Comprehension   Listening and comprehension ability continues to develop through the various read-aloud strategies outlined in Chapter

Three. Comprehension is also promoted when children respond to literature in a variety of ways as outlined in *Learning Activities for Centers* in Chapter Two, *Ways to Respond to Literature,* and during the *Shared Reading Process* in Chapter Three. More advanced listening and comprehension activities are introduced during the various guided reading strategies such as *Guided Reading with Familiar and Unfamiliar Refrain Books, Guided Reading with Familiar Complex Picture Books* (Chapter Four), and during *Activities with Information Books, Theme Studies, Author Studies* (Chapter Five).

Concepts of Books   Concepts of print materials continue to grow as children participate in many read-aloud sessions. Concepts of books are further developed during *Activities for Information Books* and *Theme Studies* (Chapter Five) where children are introduced to a variety of different forms of writing (predictable pattern books, poetry, fantasy, lists, and informational books). Children's knowledge of authors increases as they examine the styles of different writers during *Author Studies* (Chapter Five).

Reading Behaviors   Reading ability continues to expand during the various read-aloud procedures, the shared reading process, the dictated story process, and the dictated sentence procedure. Understanding of phrases and sentences is promoted during the strategy *Developing Sentence and Phrase Recognition* (Chapter Four). Children become more confident readers when they participate in the many guided reading activities such as *Guided Reading with Familiar and Unfamiliar Predictable Text* and *Guided Reading with Familiar and Unfamiliar Refrain Books* (also in Chapter Four).

Word Knowledge   Several strategies help children focus on words such as the shared reading process and the dictated sentence procedure (see Chapter Three). In addition, a special focus on recognizing words is promoted in the section *Developing Word Knowledge* where children learn words in the context of the school environment, in dictated sentences, and in pattern literature (Chapter Four). *Theme Studies* and *Author Studies* also extend understanding of words (Chapter Five).

Reading Strategies   Children in the Developing phase continue to use the semantic and syntactic cueing systems as well as the graphophonic strategy. They begin to integrate these three strategies when they read their dictated stories and during the guided reading procedures found in Chapter Four (*Guided Reading with Familiar Predictable Text, Guided Reading with Unfamiliar Predictable Text,* and *Guided Reading with Familiar and Unfamiliar Refrain Books*). They also become more familiar with phonics strategies when they participate in the strategies *Developing Letter Recognition* and *Developing Phonics Knowledge* found in Chapter Four.

Informing Parents About the Developing Phase of Reading

In order to inform parents about the Developing phase, see Parent Letter 4.

Independent Reading Phase

During this phase children's reading becomes more accomplished. The characteristics of this phase follow.

Comprehension   Learners at the Independent phase continue to benefit from having stories read to them and they are able to understand stories at more complex levels as they recall more details, ideas, and concepts in stories and develop deeper understandings of how story elements work (characters, events, problems, solutions). Children in the Independent phase also interpret stories in more complex ways through art, drama, discussions, book talks, and through dictated and written responses.

Concepts of Books   Concepts of print materials expand during this phase as children read many different genres (pattern stories, chart stories, dictated stories, refrain books, complex picture books, letters, nonfiction, fantasy, and folktales). Their knowledge of authors increases as well, and they begin to identify characteristics of familiar authors and compare the styles of various authors.

Reading Behaviors   At the Independent phase children begin to read both familiar and unfamiliar selections such as predictable pattern literature, refrain books, poetry, lists, chart stories, nonfiction, and personal dictated stories. By the end of this phase children are able to read about 20 familiar pattern selections, about ten unfamiliar pattern selections, as well as their own dictated stories. During the Independent phase children's oral reading becomes more fluid as they gain more confidence reading both familiar and unfamiliar text.

Word Knowledge   Word knowledge increases rapidly during this phase. Children are now able to sort known words in a variety of ways and create numerous word families. By the end of this phase children recognize about 100 words or more.

Reading Strategies   At this phase children begin to integrate reading strategies as they employ semantic, syntactic, and graphophonic strategies simultaneously. They also begin to self-correct errors they make in reading.

Rate of Learning   Most children reach the Independent phase sometime during first and second grade.

Developmental Reading Behavior Inventory   A comprehensive list of reading behaviors associated with the Independent phase is found in the Developmental Reading Behavior Inventory in Appendix A.

Literary Activities to Support Independent Readers

Several key strategies outlined below and in Chapters Three, Four, and Five promote reading ability during the Independent phase.

Comprehension   This is developed during the many read-aloud strategies and guided reading strategies such as *Guided Reading with Familiar and Unfamiliar Refrain Books, Guided Reading with Familiar Complex Picture Books*, and *Independent Reading Activities* (Chapter Four). Children are required to think at higher levels when they engage in the *Activities for Information Books, Theme Activities*, and *Author Studies* (Chapter Five).

Concepts of Books   Many activities help children increase their understanding of print materials when they participate in read-aloud sessions (Chapter Three), *Activities for Informational Books, Theme Studies*, and *Author Studies* (Chapter Five) where children become aware of many different genres and compare writing styles of different authors.

Reading Behaviors   As children continue to read their dictated stories and participate in the many guided reading activities, their reading ability progresses. Their independence grows as they participate in the *Independent Reading Activities* (Chapter Four) and begin to read predictable pattern selections, refrain books, and complex picture books with ease.

Word Knowledge   A number of strategies support growth in word knowledge such as reading dictated stories, participating in guided reading activities, and during *Theme Studies* and *Author Studies* (Chapter Five). Specific attention to word knowledge is found in the section *Developing Word Knowledge* (Chapter Four). Here children extend their knowledge of words in their environment, in dictated sentences, pattern books, and theme literature.

Reading Strategies   Children at the Independent phase begin to integrate the three cueing systems (semantic, syntactic, and graphophonic) as they read their dictated stories, pattern literature, refrain books, information books, theme books and books, by particular authors. Children use semantic, syntactic, and phonics strategies during the guided reading strategies in Chapter Four and during *Theme Studies* and *Author Studies* found in Chapter Five. In addition, the phonics strategy is reinforced during the strategy *Developing Phonics Knowledge* (Chapter Four).

Developmental Reading Behavior Inventory   A detailed list of reading behaviors at the various reading phases, Emergent, Beginning, Developing, and Independent is outlined in the Developmental Reading Behavior Inventory in Appendix A.

Informing Parents About the Independent Phase of Reading

In order to inform parents about the Independent phase of reading, copy and send home Parent Letter 5.

DEVELOPMENTAL READING TEST

There is no easy way to determine with any exactness when children are demonstrating behaviors in any one reading phase because children are such individuals and may demonstrate some behaviors from all four phases. However, the following procedure may give you an approximate guide regarding the phase children appear to be functioning in.

Materials for the Test

You will need the following:

1. Predictable Literature: Any predictable pattern selection can be used, or you can use the text called *The Marmalade Cat* found in Appendix B.

   Paper: any blank piece of paper will do.

   Writing implements: pencils, markers and crayons

Use the following procedure:

1. Comprehension: Read the text to the child and have them interpret the story by retelling it back to you in their own words to ensure they comprehend the text.

2. Re-reading the Text: Re-read the text in different ways:

   Adult Reads: Re-read the selection to the child while pointing to the words;

   Tandem Reading: Read the text with the child while pointing to the text;

3. Identify Text: Invite the child to read the text alone while pointing to the words.

Sentence or Phrase: Point to a predictable phrase or sentence and ask the child to read it with you and then alone;

Words: Ask the child to point to or frame any words they know in the story.

4. Reading Strategies: Ask the child to tell you what helps them read. Give them prompts by using some of the following questions.

    Semantic Questions: "Do pictures help you read?" "Do you remember parts of the story from reading it together?" "Do experiences you have had before help you with the words?"

    Syntax Questions: "Do the repeated lines help you remember the story?" "Does the refrain help you remember the words?"

    Graphophonic Questions: Point to individual words that have regular spelling and ask them to name the beginning consonant; ask the child to point to words that begin with certain consonants (b, d, l, m, s, t); ask the child to point to words that end with these same consonants.

Observations

Observe what the child does when they read alone and note their responses.

1. Independent Readers

    Children who are at the Independent phase will be able to:

    ▶ demonstrate understanding of the story by including most details of the story in the retelling;

    ▶ read the whole story fluently;

    ▶ identify most words in the story;

    ▶ correct errors made when they read;

    ▶ identify initial and final sounds in words.

2. Developing Phase

    Children in the Developing phase will be able to:

    ▶ demonstrate understanding of the story by including many details of the story in the retelling;

    ▶ read parts of the story accurately;

    ▶ read the refrain accurately;

    ▶ identify many different words in the story (15 to 20);

    ▶ may ask for help with words;

> ‣ identify some words in the story that have particular initial
> sounds.

3. Beginning Phase

   Children in the Beginning phase will be able to:

   > ‣ demonstrate understanding of the story by including many details
   >   of the story in the retelling;
   > ‣ point to words and assign an oral response (the oral response
   >   may not always match the printed word);
   > ‣ read the repeated words, lines, and refrain accurately;
   > ‣ identify a few (5 to 10) different words in the story;
   > ‣ may ask for help with words;
   > ‣ identify a few words in the story that have particular initial sounds.

4. Emergent Behaviors

   Children in the Emergent phase will be able to:

   > ‣ demonstrate understanding of the story by including some details
   >   of the story during a retelling;
   > ‣ retell much of the story from memory as though they are "reading"
   >   but do not point to any words;
   > ‣ read the refrain while the adult reads with them;
   > ‣ point to the title and illustrator but are unable to name them;
   > ‣ name a few words that begin with certain sounds but those words
   >   are not necessarily in the story.

READING APPROACHES: TRADITIONAL PHONICS AND BALANCED APPROACH

During the latter part of the twentieth century numerous debates have raged regarding how reading should be taught. Much of the discussion revolved around the use of phonics. Some researchers profess it is *the* most important strategy to use with early readers and should be used almost exclusively. Other researchers claim that phonics is less functional to early readers and should not be introduced until children have a sight vocabulary of several words. Still others believe that phonics should be integrated along with other cueing strategies such as semantics and syntax, since all three strategies are useful for beginning readers. From these debates, two main approaches to reading emerge, the Phonics approach and the Balanced approach. Of course most teachers use aspects from both approaches.

Traditional Phonics-Based Approach

In this approach much of the instruction is formal with a strong emphasis on phonics; student activities are usually worksheets that reinforce phonics concepts and reading material is based on phonics principles.

• **Sound/symbol relationships:** Teachers formally teach sound/symbol relationships very early, even before engaging children in reading stories. Children are formally taught that certain letters make corresponding sounds (*p* makes a 'puh' sound, *t* makes a 'tuh' sound, etc.).

Rules   Phonics rules are also formally taught as separate skill exercises regardless of whether children need the skills in their reading and writing.

Phonics Programs   Teachers are often required to purchase commercial phonics programs or workbooks that reinforce phonics skills. In such programs, both reading materials, teacher instruction, and learning activities are dominated by phonics.

Learning Activities   In a Traditional Phonics approach, children engage in numerous activities with the sole purpose of reinforcing phonics concepts. These activities are usually taught as isolated skills, frequently with no connection to stories children read or compose. Phonics concepts are reinforced by having children circle pictures that begin with particular sound/symbols (circle pictures that begin with *s* such as *swing*, *sandwich*, *sun*). Children draw pictures of things that begin with *t* (*toys*, *telephone*, *table*, or *T.V.*) and draw pictures of things that end with *d* (*dad*, *rod*, *weed*, *mud*). Teachers invite children to name things that begin with *p* (*pet*, *pony*, *pictures*, *pan*) or end with *p* (*hop*, *tap*, *step*, *help*) and these words are recorded on charts. Children apply their phonics knowledge by making lists of words that have similar sound/symbol relationships: *at* family (*cat*, *mat*, *rat*, *fat*, *sat*); *un* family (*run*, *bun*, *sun*, *fun*).

Reading Material   Reading material in this approach is usually limited to phonically regular texts, which are carefully written with only phonics principles in mind. Text is usually built around phonic word families. For example, a book may use a predominance of words containing the short vowel sound of *a* (*cat*, *sat*, *mat*, *hat*). The text may read, *Dan has a hat. Dan sat on the hat. The hat is flat. Dan is sad.* Notice that most of the words in this passage are phonically regular and include the short vowel *a*. These texts are usually written by personnel who work for commercial reading programs rather than authentic authors of picture books. In the Phonics approach children are often required to read phonically regular texts for several years before they are introduced to authentic literature with rich language and meaningful story lines.

Concerns with a Phonics Only Approach

In a predominantly Phonics approach, the study of phonics permeates all aspects of learning to the exclusion of many other equally important strategies, such as reading good literature, developing understanding and comprehension, as well as using other cueing strategies such as semantics and syntax as well as graphophonics. Specific concerns follow.

Isolated Skill Instruction

While most educators agree that phonics concepts are important in learning to read, many believe that children retain phonic information better when phonics skills are learned in some context that is meaningful to them such as their reading material (literature, chart stories, dictated stories, and sentence strips). An extensive review of the research literature by Margaret Moustafa (1997) revealed that children employ the phonics strategy more effectively when they use their knowledge of known words from familiar contexts as the basis for helping them pronounce words they don't recognize. In fact, Jacobson (1998) suggests "if children are subjected to heavy doses of sounding out words in isolation—in other words, decoding words in workbooks and not in stories—they may place too much emphasis on this one strategy. They may read word by word without fluency or attention to meaning" (p. 77).

Rules   Although many phonics rules are reliable and should be taught in some way, of the approximate 110 phonics rules, few are applicable 100 percent of the time.

Reading Material   While phonically regular reading material is relatively easy to read, these stories cannot really be called literature because of the contrived vocabulary. Phonic reading material often lacks complex story structures, interesting vocabulary, and compelling story lines. Moreover, phonic-based reading material generally fails to include a variety of different writing forms and genres. Reading too much of this kind of material could give children the mistaken idea that reading is uninteresting and boring. Therefore, these books should be used sparingly. Moreover, when phonically regular reading material dominates children's reading time, children run the risk of replacing important literary experiences such as reading good literature, chart stories, and dictated stories.

Meaning   Reading too much phonically regular text also reduces children's ability to get meaning from stories since phonically regular stories do not make much sense. Consequently, children's thinking is not challenged since the phonic-based reading material provides little on which to reflect, respond, or interpret.

Cueing Systems   Finally, when only one of the cueing systems (graphophonic) is emphasized at the expense of others, as is so often the case in the Phonics approach, children are disadvantaged since they are seldom instructed on how to employ other equally important reading strategies such as semantic (meaning) and syntax (order of words).

Informing Parents About Phonics Approaches to Reading

Parent Letter 6 outlines the principles and practices of the Phonics approach to reading.

Balanced Reading Approach

At the heart of a Balanced reading approach is authentic literature, gaining meaning and understanding, contextual instruction and learning, and the integration of cueing strategies.

Reading Material   In a Balanced language program, quality literature selections are the main sources for reading instruction. Several types of literature are used such as predictable pattern literature, poetry, songs, refrain books, complex picture books, and informational material. Quality literature introduces children to varieties of forms of print material (narratives, poetry, fantasy, nonfiction), rich and varied vocabulary, a variety of authors, and information to satisfy children's interests. Experiences with good literature help children gain meaning about characters, events, problems, and resolutions. Reading material with a literature base is more interesting, more complex, and filled with more information than text in phonically regular texts predominantly used in the Traditional Phonics approach.

Children experience quality literature in a number of ways: when it is read to them, when they hear quality literature at the listening center, when they read along with teachers and other adults, and when they begin to read literature independently.

In addition, a Balanced approach uses children's own language by inviting them to dictate stories about their own unique experiences. Dictated stories also contain more complex language than phonically regular selections so often used in the Phonics approach.

Meaning   Meaning is paramount in a Balanced approach. Thus, children are introduced to literature well before they can read for themselves.

As children listen to a variety of literature they first gain an overall under-standing of stories. From stories they hear, they discover what characters do, how they act, the problems they encounter, and how they resolve them. Comprehension is further developed through questioning and when children interpret stories through storytelling, art, drama, and writing.

Contextual Instruction and Learning   Another feature of a Balanced approach is that instruction is conducted in the context of meaningful print such as literature or personally dictated stories. As children listen to stories, they also learn a number of concepts of print such as titles, authors, how pages are turned, direction of print, and so on. During several readings and re-readings, children soon recall the repeated lines, phrases, sentences re-frains, individual words, and finally, sound/symbol relationships.

Reading Strategies   In a Balanced approach several reading strategies are employed (semantics, syntax, and graphophonics), as children learn to read rather than the phonics strategy alone as in the Phonics approach.

• Semantics: One of the first cueing systems children employ is seman-tics or meaning strategies. Here, they rely on memory of stories that they have heard many times. They also use pictures to help them get mean-ing from text. In fact, many children "read" pictures in books even be-fore they attend to print. As children orally "read" familiar stories themselves, they frequently use much of the vocabulary in the text and occasionally substitute different language for other words. For example, the text may have the word *rabbit* but some children may substitute the word *bunny*. Because the alternative word (*bunny*) retains the overall meaning of the story, we shouldn't panic because we know that chil-dren are reading for understanding. In other words, the substituted text still makes sense. Another valuable semantic strategy is informed guess-ing when encountering an unknown word. Research suggests that intel-ligent guessing based on other information in the text or illustrations is a good strategy to use. For example, when a little girl sees a door with a picture of someone wearing a skirt and the word *ladies* in print and says "This is the women's washroom, right, Dad?" she is using semantic strategies (pictures and print) to figure out that this is the correct wash-room to use. Reading for meaning is a strategy children and adults use throughout their reading experiences. During the Emergent and Begin-ning phases of reading, children rely mainly on semantics (meaning) to make sense of stories. Their memory of stories that have been read to them many times helps them reconstruct stories for retelling. You can observe the semantic strategy at work when young children turn pages of picture books and make up reasonable stories to correspond to the illustrations, while still keeping the meaning of the text.

• Syntax: Another cueing system children employ very early is syntax, the natural patterns of words, sentences, and phrases in stories. Children rely on syntax to read the repeated lines in predictable pattern literature. This is one of the reasons why pattern literature is frequently used for early reading instruction. For example, children find it easier to read stories that have repeated refrains, sentences, phrases, and words and are quickly able to read these repeated sections fluently. Emergent and Beginning readers generally rely on meaning (context) and patterns (syntax) before they become aware of the graphophonic strategy.

• Graphophonic: The graphophonic cueing system is also a useful strategy in learning to read when it is employed along with semantics and syntax. However, young children usually do not employ this strategy until the Beginning and Developing phases of reading. The graphophonic strategy is especially useful for words that have consistent sound/symbol relationships, about half the words in English (*hat, him, bet, top, cut*). However, for the other 50 percent of the English language, children need to employ combinations of semantic, syntactic, and graphophonic strategies in order to make sense of words like *night, come, love, cough*, for example. Margaret Moustafa (1997) contends that children employ phonic principles to learn new words when they use rimes in known words as a guide to figure out unknown vocabulary with the same rime. For example, once a child recognizes the word *black*, they are better able to learn new words containing the same rime (*ack*) in words such as *tack, rack, back, Jack, Mack*, and *sack*.

Integrated Cueing Systems   In a Balanced reading approach, children engage in all three cueing systems simultaneously as they are involved in rich experiences in language such as singing songs, listening to quality literature, reading authentic literature, dictating personal stories, and writing their own compositions.

Informing Parents About a Balanced Approach to Reading

Help parents understand the value of a Balanced approach to reading by copying Parent Letter 7.

Using the Three Cueing Systems

We can help children use the three cueing systems when they read in the following ways:

Semantics   When children are "stuck" on words, ask questions that address meaning (semantics): "What word would make sense here?" "Look at the pictures for ideas."

Syntax   Ask questions that get children thinking about patterns of language (syntax) in stories: Ask, "Is there a pattern in the story that can help you with this word?" What kind of word makes sense here—the name of an object or an action?

Graphophonics   In addition to asking semantic and syntactical questions, also ask children to think about sounds in words: Ask, "What sound does this beginning letter make? What sound does the ending letter make?" Phonics questions should only be asked, however, when words in question have phonetically regular spelling (*can, but, pet, in, hop*). When children come across unknown words containing rimes in words they know, help them make the connection between the known and unknown words. For instance, when the child hesitates on the word *tame*, say something like, "Think about the word *came* that you read earlier. *Came* has the same rime as *tame*. You know the sound the letter *T* makes. Now can you figure out what the word *tame* is?" The phonics strategy is less helpful for words that have irregular spellings (*through, fight, station*), which represent about 50 percent of English words. For these irregular spellings, semantic and syntactic strategies are more useful.

Integration of Cueing Strategies   Research claims that learning to read is more effective when all three cueing strategies, semantics (meaning), syntax (pattern), and graphophonics (sound/symbol relationships), are employed in concert with one another. As well, children learn these strategies more easily as they are reading stories rather than completing isolated skill exercises as in the Traditional Phonics approach. Learning words, letters, and sound/symbols as isolated activities, as in the Traditional Phonics approach, have less meaning for young children learning to read.

Informing Parents About Integrating Reading Strategies

Parent Letter 8 discusses how reading strategies can be integrated.

To sum up, compared to the Traditional Phonics approach, the Balanced approach employs reading material that is more meaningful, complex, interesting, and contains more information than phonics-based reading material. In the Balanced approach, reading instruction is conducted within the context of reading real, authentic literature right from the start, rather than learning graphophonic skills through isolated drills. In the Balanced approach children are expected to think about and understand events and complex relationships between characters, their problems, events they experience, and solutions they choose; whereas, reading material in the Traditional Phonics approach contains little to reflect upon or think about. While both approaches value phonics instruction, in the Balanced approach phonics is taught in the context of quality reading material by starting with words children already know in stories they have heard, read in unison, and read alone; while in the Traditional Phonics approach, graphophonic relationships are pretaught *before* children are expected to read passages of text. Finally, in the Balanced approach three cueing systems are employed, while in the Traditional Phonics approach emphasizes *only* the graphophonics strategy.

In Chapter Two I will discuss ways to organize the classroom in order to implement a Balanced approach to reading instruction.

2

Organizing the Classroom

ENVIRONMENTS THAT PROMOTE LITERACY

When organizing a classroom to promote literacy, teachers must take into account the physical, social/emotional, and academic needs of young children as outlined in Chapter One. Since children need to socialize, talk, move about, listen to stories, read, and write, classrooms set up in learning centers seem to accommodate these needs best. Organizing the room into centers also provides more space for movement, which is so necessary for the physical development of early years children. For example, a reading corner is set up for children to look at and read books; a listening center is organized where children can listen to all sorts of print material; drama materials are found in another corner so children can plan dramatizations and perform puppet shows; at a composing center dictated stories are composed and recorded on a regular basis; in an art corner easels are erected so children can paint and draw pictures to respond to literature they hear and read; writing implements and paper are placed at the writing center; and science and social studies centers contain artifacts and re-source materials to reflect various thematic units of study. In addition, most early years classrooms are equipped with building blocks, sand boxes, and water centers to develop mathematics and science concepts. A large carpeted space is used for whole class gatherings and children's desks are grouped in clusters of four to six in order to make space for the various learning centers. Some teachers prefer tables and skip assigned desks altogether.

Much of the room preparations are made during the summer months before the children arrive. Following are detailed descriptions of several learning centers mentioned previously, including materials required to make them functional.

Gathering Area

Teachers usually plan for a large area in the classroom for the whole class to gather for various activities such as reading aloud, shared reading sessions, developing chart stories, sharing time, and celebrations.

• **Materials required:** A large carpet helps to define this space and at the same time provides children with a comfortable place to sit. A rocking chair placed in a corner is used by teachers to conduct various whole class activities. Children enjoy sitting on the rocking chair too for sharing their accomplishments. A chart stand and magic markers or chalkboard are close by for composing chart stories and making Big Books. Literature selections are displayed in a prominent place, and walls around the gathering area are filled with chart stories, Big Books, songs, and word charts.

Reading Corner

The reading corner is one of the most important learning centers and requires careful planning.

Materials   In the reading corner place cushions, beanbag chairs, or small sofas on a small area carpet where children can sit, sprawl out, or lay on their tummies to read and look at books. Set the reading corner near shelves and counters so books can be displayed attractively as an invitation to read them. Invite parent volunteers to work in this center to read to children and to listen to them read.

Print Selections   Display books of various genres (songs, poetry, wordless books, pattern books, Big Books, complex picture books, folktales, class charts, informational material) at many levels of difficulty. Display selections so children can see the covers, but also have many housed in

small bins coded according to difficulty or subject. Also display familiar chart stories, Big Books, and selections that were used in previous read-aloud and shared reading sessions.

Selecting Books   Before encouraging children to look at or read books in the reading corner, they may require minilessons on how to select books. Here are some ideas first graders have suggested.

• Find books that are familiar to you from read-aloud sessions or when you made Big Books;

• Ask friends for selections they liked;

• Find books by authors you like;

• Choose books based on topics you are interested in;

• Check for interesting pictures in books to give you an idea if you might like looking at the book;

• Find books that are easy to read. If there are too many words you are unsure of, put it back and find an easier one;

• Put a book back if it is not interesting to you and find another one that is.

Recording Books Read   Have each child record the stories they have read into a reading log. (See page 126 for an example.)

Activities for Responding to Books   Children learn so much from simply looking at and reading books, so provide lots of uninterrupted time just to read and enjoy books. Occasionally introduce the children to different ways to respond to the books they read. Requesting a response to a single book while at the reading center is appropriate even though they will likely have looked at or read several books. Find more response ideas in the section *Learning Activities for Centers* in Chapter Two and in the section *Ways to Respond to Literature* outlined in Chapter Three. Several response activities are also listed at the end of this section. Give children choices regarding how they will respond.

Listening Center

The listening center is a place where children hear familiar and new stories to reinforce both listening and reading skills:

Materials and Resources Required   At the listening center, place a tape recorder and several earphones as well as numerous audiotaped stories on cassettes. Include audiotapes of both pattern selections as well as complex picture books with high density print. When text sets (several copies of a single title) are available that correspond with audiotapes, children are able to follow along in their own copy.

Obtaining Audiotapes   Audiotapes can be purchased but you can also make your own by audiotaping yourself during read-aloud sessions.

Reading buddies in grades four to eight are also able to make wonderful audiotapes. Ask their teachers to make this into an oral reading assignment.

Listening Center Activities   Invite children to participate in *one* activity after they listen to a selection in order to enhance their listening skills. Several listening activities are listed at the end of this section.

Drama/Speaking Center

The drama center is an ideal place for children to develop their speaking ability and to develop deeper understandings of literature.

Materials and Resources Required   At the drama center have a box of props such as old wigs, hats, large pieces of fabric that can be used for cloaks, tents, shawls, magic capes, and blankets. Children also love old telephones and implements that can be used for magic wands. Have lots of familiar literature selections available that children have heard before during read-aloud sessions as a focus for their dramatizations.

Reading   Invite the children to choose a familiar selection and re-read it together before planning their dramatization.

Drama Activities   Several drama activities are listed at the end of this section.

Dictated Story Center

Dictating stories is a wonderful way to develop children's concepts of narratives and to extend their ability in speaking and composing. Completed dictated stories also provide meaningful reading material.

Materials and Resources Required   Children bring their own personal dictated story booklets to the center (20 pages of unlined paper stapled between manilla covers). However, it is a good idea to also have loose papers or small empty story booklets available for children who want to publish dictated stories. Have pencils and thin magic markers available for recording stories as well as crayons and markers for illustrating them. Invite parent volunteers or reading buddies to record children's stories. After the dictated story is complete, the volunteer reads the story back to the child before they illustrate it. See Chapter Three for dictation procedures.

Dictated Story Center Activities   Several dictated story activities are listed at the end of this section.

Art Center

One of the most effective ways to interpret literature and to note whether children understand stories is by examining their art. Art is also integrated with literature study when children illustrate their Big Books. For example, *Whose Mouse Are You?* by Robert Krause (2000) was illustrated with crayon by Wayne Gingrich's class while the children in Wendy Brum's first-grade class illustrated *One Bright Monday Morning* by Aline and Joseph

Baum (1973) with multimedia (painted background and colored construction paper for characters and scenery). Children enjoy working with several different types of art media, so every second week or so change the media at the art center. Consider placing the art center close to cupboards and a sink for easy cleanup.

Painting Center At the painting center set up easels or put large heavy plastic sheets on the floor on which children paint. Young children need large pieces of paper for their pictures (18″ × 24″) to accommodate for their immature muscle development. Put the paint into small containers or muffin tins and have several paint brushes available. A couple of large containers of water should be set out for washing paint brushes before

using different colors. Prevent paint from getting on children's clothing by having them wear old shirts, smocks, or plastic garbage bags.

Drawing Center   Materials for a drawing center include paper of all sizes and colors and lots of crayons, washable markers, colored chalk, and crayon pastels.

Paper Collage Center   At this center provide all kinds of different colored paper of different textures (tissue paper, construction paper, manilla paper) and creative construction materials such as paper rolls, bits of lace, fabric, and buttons. Also provide pencils, scissors, and glue.

Puppet Center   Resources required for the puppet center include materials to make particular kinds of puppets:

- *Stick puppets:* In order to make stick puppets you will need to have many pieces of different colored paper, scissors, glue, markers, crayons, and sticks on which to attach the two-dimensional figures.

- *Cylinder puppets:* Decorate toilet paper or paper towel rolls with construction paper, fabric, felt, and buttons.

- *Paper plate puppets:* For paper plate puppets, children will need different sizes of white paper plates, a variety of different colored pieces of construction paper, tissue paper, fabric, buttons, crayons, markers, glue, scissors, and sticks such as rulers or popsicle sticks to hold the puppets.

- *Paper bag puppets:* In order to make paper bag puppets have several different sized paper bags available and newspaper to use for stuffing them. Have on hand a variety of colored paper, fabric scraps, felt, buttons, scissors, glue, crayons, and colored markers.

- *Sock puppets:* To make sock puppets you will need several old socks, stuffing for them (newspaper, panty hose), and material to decorate them such as fabric bits, felt, buttons, and construction paper.

Modeling Center

Modeling with plasticine or play dough is a great way to develop fine muscle control that is so important in the physical development of early years children.

Materials and Resources Required   For modeling, have fresh plasticine, play dough, or clay available. Cover the table with heavy plastic in order to protect it and for easy cleanup.

Art Activities   Various art activities are listed at the end of this section.

Writing Center

The writing center is usually set up on a table or on a cluster of desks. It is a place where children compose their own stories. Set up a writing center at the beginning of the year if you are comfortable with allowing children to use any symbols they know to record their stories (scribbles, invented marks). Teachers also need to be tolerant of children's approximate spellings (*bkoz* for *because*) as they use their phonics skills to guide their spelling. Teachers who are uncomfortable with unconventional symbols and spelling are wise to set up the writing center later in the year.

Materials and Resources   At the writing center provide lots of instruments for recording stories (pencils, crayons, markers), many types of paper of different size and color, booklets of blank unlined paper with construction paper covers, and blank strips of paper ($6'' \times 18''$) on which to print sentences (sentence strips). Unlined paper works best with very young children since they often do not have the physical dexterity to print between lines. Mary Ellen Jacobi suggests that early primary children keep their work better organized when they write in teacher-made notebooks of several pages (20) of unlined sheets with manilla covers. Other materials useful at the writing center are scissors, staplers, and glue.

Writing Center Activities   Several writing activities are listed at the end of this section.

Handwriting Center

The handwriting center helps children develop their fine muscles to manipulate pencils and crayons with more control.

Materials and Resources   At the handwriting center provide numerous laminated sentences or phrases from predictable pattern literature or child-composed sentences. Print these onto sentence strips ($6'' \times 18''$). Also have crayons and washable markers at the center.

Handwriting Activities   Have children copy over the teacher's print with washable markers; also have them copy under the teacher's print.

We went to the mall last night.

We went to the mall last night.
We went to the mall last night

Word Study Center

The word study center helps children become familiar with individual words.

Materials and Resources   At this center have many familiar sentence strips of repeated sentences from predictable pattern literature that were read to the children during read-aloud sessions and during the shared reading process. Cut up words to match these sentences. Also set out familiar chart stories, word cards, magazines, newspapers, blank paper, plus washable markers, scissors, and glue.

Word Study Center Activities   Many activities to develop understandings of words are listed at the end of this section.

LEARNING ACTIVITIES FOR CENTERS

The following learning activities at the various centers will extend children's literacy development. They can be assigned to each group of children at a particular center or lists of the activities can be placed onto charts for children to select themselves.

Reading Center Activities

Children respond to literature they read in a number of ways: Invite them to respond in *one* of the following activities:

- *Looking at books:* Look at a book and tell a story based on the pictures.

- *Illustrations and stories:* Dictate a story by using illustrations in the book as a guide.

- *Telling about it:* Tell a friend about the book.

- *Book talk:* Invite children to give a book talk to a small group telling the things they enjoyed about the book and the things they disliked.

- *Book share:* Have a book talk with a friend and tell them about the book you read and invite them to tell you about a book they liked.

- *Retelling:* Retell the story to a friend, volunteer, or reading buddy.

- *Chart reading:* With a friend, read a group chart related to a theme or author.

- *Big Book:* Read a familiar Big Book with a friend.

- *Acetate stories:* Invite children to practice their reading of stories teachers have copied onto overhead acetates.

- *Poetry:* Read a poem with a friend; use lots of expression.

- *Dictated stories:* Read a story you have dictated to a volunteer.

- *Story mapping:* Draw various events that happened in the story.

- *Picture book:* Make a picture book of the characters and some events in the story.

- *Book discussion:* Work with a volunteer and discuss *one* of these questions:

    Talk about a character you liked.

    Compare two different characters to see how they are similar and different.

    In what ways does this story remind you of something that has happened to you?

    How are the problems in this story like the problems in other stories you have read?

- *Response journals:* Respond to a book you have read by dictating or writing responses to it. Tell what you enjoyed about the story, what you learned from this story and things you would change if you were the author of this story. This activity is reserved for children who are reading independently.

Listening Center Activities

Children learn many skills as they participate in various listening activities. Choose *one* of the following activities:

- *Following along:* Listen to an audiotape of a familiar predictable pattern selection and follow along with the text on corresponding Big Books or the original commercial book.

- *Following picture books:* Listen to audiotapes of picture books and follow along with the text.

- *Characters:* Listen for characters in the story and draw one of them.

- *Events:* Listen for events in the story and draw an event.

- *Problems:* Listen for problems in the story and discuss them in your group.

- *Comparing:* With a partner, talk about the differences between two characters.

Drama/Speaking Center Activities

Children improve their speaking ability through drama and speaking activities. Through drama they demonstrate their understanding of stories they read or hear. Invite children to participate in *one* of the following activities when they are at this center.

- *Role play:* Children work in partners to role play two characters from a familiar story.

- *Telephone conversation:* With a partner, role play a telephone conversation between you and the author and tell the 'author' what you liked or didn't like about the story. Telephone a character and tell them what you liked about them.

- *Act out:* As a group, act out an event from a familiar story.

- *Act out a scene:* Use materials from the dress-up box as props to dramatize a scene from a familiar story.

- *Charades:* Play charades by making actions of a character and having the rest of the group guess who it is.

- *Mime:* Mime a situation in a story and have the group guess the story.

- *Puppet play:* Children make puppets from paper plates, bags, or socks and act out a scene from a familiar story.

- *Commercial:* With a partner, plan a commercial for radio or T.V. to advertize this book. Act out your commercial on the school P.A. or during a library class.

- *Announcement:* With a partner, plan a commercial that you perform in front of your group or on the school P.A. system.

Art Center Activities

Through art activities children show their understanding of stories as they draw characters, events, and problems. Encourage them to participate in *one* of the following activities:

- *Drawing:* Draw a picture about a favorite part of a familiar story. Using crayons, markers, or chalk pastels, draw a character that was important to you in a familiar story.
- *Story map:* Draw a story map with a friend of several events in a familiar story.
- *Paint:* Paint a picture of a character, a favorite scene, a funny part of the story, a sad part, or scarey part.
- *Picture collage:* Using magazine pictures or construction paper, cut or tear paper to create a character or scene from a theme-related story.
- *Mobile:* Using construction paper, make several characters from a familiar story and attach them with string to a coat hanger.
- *Flannel board:* Prepare scenes of a favorite story by cutting out characters and scenery from felt and placing them onto the flannel board.
- *Modeling:* With clay, play dough, or plasticine model a character from a familiar story.
- *Puppets:* Using paper bags, paper plates, or boxes, make a favorite character in a book.

Dictated Story Center Activities

Dictating stories is another way children share what they know about books they listen to or read for themselves.

- Dictate your own rendition based on a book you liked.
- Dictate captions for paintings and models you made based on a literature selection.
- Dictate sentence strips of some events in stories and copy over the teacher's print with crayon;
- Dictate sentences about a story and copy under the print;
- Dictate what you remember about the story and read it with a parent volunteer or reading buddy.
- Dictate a new story about a topic related to the theme;
- Dictate a new episode for the story;
- Dictate a new version of a story by changing the characters.

Writing Center Activities

Children also communicate their interpretations of literature by writing their own responses. Invite children to participate in *one* of the following activities:

- *Labeling:* Cut out objects related to the theme "Pets" (*dogs, cats, gold-fish*) and label them.

- *New story:* Compose a new story based on a piece of literature using all the skills you know in spelling. Try to spell as best you can and don't bother other people to help with spelling words.

- *Menu:* Create a menu for a character in a familiar story.

- *Recipe:* With a friend write a recipe for some food a character would like.

- *Lists:* Make a list of all the characters in the story.

- *Postcard:* Write a postcard to a character or author telling them what you liked or disliked.

- *Thank-you note:* Write a thank-you note to the author for writing such a good book.

- *Bumper sticker:* Compose a bumper sticker to advertize a favorite book.

Handwriting Center Activities

The following handwriting activities help young children develop fine muscle control and at the same time make them aware of sentences, words, and letters.

- *Sentence strip activities:* Copy over sentence strips of repeated lines from predictable pattern selections that have been printed by the teacher onto sentence strips (6" × 18").

- *Under-copying:* Copy under familiar sentences from pattern literature that have been printed onto sentence strips by the teacher.

Word Center Activities

The following activities help children become familiar with individual words. Invite them to participate in *one* of the activities while at this center.

- *Characters:* Frame names of characters in the story.
- *Action words:* Frame action words in a familiar chart story.

- *Descriptive words:* Frame descriptive words in a familiar literature selection.

- *Word cards:* Cut out pictures to match the theme words on cards (farm animals: *horse, pig, duck*).

- *Word sorting:* Sort word cards according to type of animal (*farm animals, woodland animals, pets*).

- *Word sorting:* Sort words from familiar Big Books according to action words, things, colors, etc.

- *Finding words:* Circle all the words you know on a page of newspaper or magazine.

- *Beginning sounds:* Frame words that begin with certain sound /symbols.

- *Ending sounds:* Frame words that end with particular sound/symbols.

- *I Spy:* Play "I Spy" with a friend to identify words from a familiar Big Book that begin with certain sounds and end with particular sounds.

- *Sound/symbols:* On a magazine page, circle all the words that begin with a particular letter at the beginning of an animal theme word d̲uck (*dog, donkey, down*); circle words that end with the sound like the end of an animal theme word cat̲ (*sit, rabbit, goat*).

Informing Parents About Learning Centers

Copy and send home Parent Letter 9, which outlines the value of learning centers in early years classrooms.

LITERATURE THAT DEVELOPS LITERACY

Several types of literature are valuable for developing literacy in early years programs. They include predictable pattern literature, refrain books, complex picture books, and nonfiction materials.

Building the Foundation for Reading

Predictable pattern literature is extremely valuable for reading aloud to children, for developing comprehension, for developing concepts of print, for independent reading material, and for building the foundation for writing new stories based on predictable structures.

Characteristics   Predictable pattern literature selections are easily identified because they usually contain bright pictures, large print, and few lines of print per page. Predictable pattern literature may also have rhyme, rhythm, repeated words, phrases, sentences, and refrains.

Value of Predictable Literature

• **Concepts of print:** Predictable literature is valuable in learning to read because it can be introduced to children well before they are able to understand concepts of print or can read for themselves. Babies at two or three months respond to predictable literature being read to them; they look at the bright pictures and enjoy the rhythmic patterns. In fact, parents report that reading to their infants often settles them down when they are fussy. Before the age of one year, babies begin to respond to text that is read to them by making sounds of animals in stories and moving like characters. Babies even have favorite books that they enjoy looking at frequently. As babies and toddlers listen to literature, they hear complex language and at the same time are learning numerous concepts portrayed in the literature itself.

• **Predictable literature and oral language:** When babies are read to from birth, they discover that stories are enjoyable and fun to hear. The language children hear in literature expands their oral language since language patterns in literature are more complex than the oral language they hear from family members. Indeed, toddlers' first words are frequently those introduced in literature.

- **Predictable literature and reading:** Although they are not conscious of it, toddlers also gradually become aware of conventions of print: those black marks on the page seem to carry the same message; they notice that pages are turned in the same order; as parents point to text, toddlers internalize that text moves from left to right and across the page.

- **Predictable literature and young readers:** Predictable pattern literature is particularly useful for reading aloud for enjoyment as well as for reading instruction. Reading predictable literature builds understanding, makes children aware of the structure of stories, extends their knowledge of the world, increases their oral vocabulary, and draws their attention to the finer features of text such as sentences, phrases, words, and letters.

- **Predictable literature and composing:** Many of the features in predictable literature are good models for young children to use as guides for composing stories themselves. At first, new versions of predictable selections are dictated by the children, but as children begin to read, they are able to compose predictable versions on their own.

Informing Parents About the Value of Reading Predictable Text

Parent Letter 10 discusses the value of reading predictable texts to young children.

Types of Predictable Pattern Literature

There are numerous types of predictable literature such as wordless books, books with repeated lines, selections with rhyme, sequential pattern books, and cumulative sequence books. Gail Tompkins (1998) describes several kinds of predictable pattern literature.

Wordless Books   Wordless books are books that tell an entire story through illustrations. The absence of words allows children to focus their whole attention on the illustrations to communicate the story rather than words. The illustrations carry the story and its setting, characters, events, problems, and resolutions.

- **Value of Wordless Books:** Using wordless books in the early years is particularly useful for emergent readers because children can develop their oral storytelling skills to describe the people, places, and actions depicted in the illustrations. Reading wordless books also gives them the chance to apply their knowledge of story structures they have learned while listening to stories during read-aloud sessions.

- **Wordless Book Selections:** In Appendix D is a list of wordless books young children enjoy.

Repetition Books   Some books have phrases and sentences that are repeated over and over. Two books by Bill Martin Jr. are classic pattern books that employ repeated patterns. They are *Brown Bear, Brown Bear, What Do You See?* (1983) and *Polar Bear, Polar Bear, What Do You Hear?* (1991). The repeated patterns in both stories make the selections easy for young children to remember. Additional pattern literature selections are listed in Appendix D.

Rhyme and Rhythm Selections

Rhyme and rhythm in books also help children predict text. Nursery rhymes typically incorporate rhyme and rhythm. Look for books of nursery rhymes such as Tomie de Paola's *Mother Goose* (1985); *My Very First Mother Goose* by Iona Opie (1996); *Alligator Pie* (Denis Lee, 1987); *The Ice Cream Store* (Denis Lee, 1991); *Poetry Party* (Bruce Lansky, 1996); or *Falling Up* (Shel Silverstein, 1996). See Appendix D for several selections that have rhyming features.

Sequential Pattern Books   Some books use a familiar sequence such as logical events, days of the week, months of the year, numbers, and letters in the alphabet to structure the text. Three books by Donald Crews use a sequential structure. They are *Freight Train* (1978), *Flying* (1989), and *Sail Away* (1995). These books are particularly appealing to young readers because of the minimal print per page and the bright illustrations that support the text. A list of additional sequential pattern selections is found in Appendix D.

Cumulative Pattern Books   In cumulative pattern books particular sentences and phrases are repeated and expanded in each episode. One of my favorite cumulative selections is *The Cake That Mack Ate*, by Rose Robart (1986), which is based on *The House That Jack Built* (Peppe, 1985). The pattern in this book repeats the line *the cake that Mack ate* in each refrain (*This is the hen that laid the egg that went into the cake that Mack ate*). In Appendix D is a list of cumulative pattern literature.

Literature with Refrains, Complex Picture Books, Issue Books, and Nonfiction

Refrain Books   Refrain books are a type of literature that incorporates a repeated stanza, chorus, or refrain throughout the piece. For the most part, refrain books have more dense print on each page and fewer illustrations than predictable pattern literature. Two types of refrain books are described in this handbook. The first type is called easy-read refrain books and the second is called traditional refrain books.

- Easy-Read Refrain Books: Easy-read refrain books have more print on each page, and there is more interaction between the characters, events, and problems compared to most predictable pattern books. But like predictable pattern literature and traditional refrain books, they have repeated refrains throughout the story. Compared to traditional refrain books, easy-read refrain books have less dense print per page and more illustrations. Some of my favorite easy-read refrain books are, *Hattie and the Fox* by Mem Fox (1992); *Mortimer* by Robert Munsch (1985) and *Peace at Last* by Jill Murphy (1980).

- Traditional Refrain Books: Traditional refrain books have more print on each page, fewer illustrations, and more complex story structures than easy-read refrain books. Characteristically, in traditional refrain books characters are usually animals, characters come in sets of three (three bears, three pigs), characters are mainly good or bad (trolls, wolves), there are usually three episodes in the story, and the refrain is repeated over and over. Favorite traditional refrain books include the *Three Bears* (Galdone, 1972) and *The Three Little Pigs* (Reinl, 1983).

- Ability to Read Refrain Books: Children in the Emergent and Beginning phases of reading are not usually able to read refrain books independently because of the difficult vocabulary. However, they often are able to read the traditional refrains themselves ("I'll huff and I'll puff and I'll blow your house in") because of the predictable syntax. However, despite the fact that young children may not be able to read refrain books independently, they are able to understand the events, problems, and endings when refrain books are read to them. In other words, refrain books are aimed at youngsters' listening levels rather than their levels of comprehension and understanding as they begin to read stories independently. Many children are able to read refrain books when they reach the Independent phase of reading. Several refrain books are listed in Appendix D.

Complex Picture Books   Compared to predictable pattern literature and refrain books, complex picture books have more complex story structures, more words on each page, illustrations expand the text rather than corresponding to it, individual sentences are longer and more complex, the font of print is smaller, and more background of information is required to understand these books.

- *Ability to read:* Complex picture books are usually read to early years youngsters because they are able to comprehend the concepts at a listening level of comprehension. Many are not able to read complex picture books until they reach the Independent phase. Complex picture books suitable for young children's listening levels are noted in Appendix D.

Issue Books   Issue books are a type of complex picture book that explore issues in children's lives, their community, and society. Issue books sensitively introduce children to ethical and social justice issues such as name-calling, bullying, racial prejudice, gender, preserving the environment, cruelty to animals, death, homelessness, and poverty. Like complex picture books, issue books usually have dense print on each page, feature fewer illustrations than in predictable pattern selections, and the story line is complex. For these reasons, issue books are intended to be read to children. Although the text is usually too complex for young children to read independently, children are able to understand the concepts at their listening level of comprehension. Most young children will find that the following issue books will cause them to think more thoughtfully about their community and the world around them. They are *Horace and Morris But Mostly Dolores* by James Howe (1999), which deals with the issue of gender; *Like Jake and Me* by Mavis Jukes (1984) is a gentle story about a young boy and his relationship with his stepfather; *The World That Jack Built* by Ruth Brown (1992) draws attention to pollution in the environment; and *Fly Away Home* by Eve Bunting (1991) explores issues of homelessness. Additional issue books are listed in Appendix D.

Nonfiction Materials   Young children enjoy reading informational material especially when it relates to their personal interests. My granddaughter Amy has loved bugs since she was a toddler, so we provide her with lots of books dealing with insects. Fortunately, there are many nonfiction books written about insects (*It's a Good Thing There Are Insects*, Fowler, 1990; *Spiders*, Gibbons, 1993; *Ladybug*, Watts, 1987). There is also good information about insects in stories generally considered fictional. For example, Eric Carle's books describe adventures of particular insects, and also provide loads of information about the insects themselves (see *The Very Hungry Caterpillar*, 1994; *The Very Quiet Cricket*, 1990; *The Very Lonely Firefly*, 1995; *The Very Busy Spider*, 1984).

• *Ability to read:* When informational selections have minimal print per page and have repeated lines and refrains, many youngsters are able to read them. However, most informational selections should be read to young children because of the difficult vocabulary. Appendix D lists several informational selections young children enjoy.

Informing Parents About Literature with Refrain Books, Complex Picture Books, Issue Books, and Nonfiction

Inform parents about the kind of literature you use in your classroom and ask them to contribute selections if they can. See Parent Letter 11.

HOW TO OBTAIN LITERATURE SELECTIONS

There are several ways to obtain literature selections for early reading instruction.

1. *School Funds for Books:* First, purchase as many new books as possible from school budgets so that quality is always maintained. Seek funds for new books from your principal and make deals and trade-offs. For example, purchase fewer selections of commercial reading programs, spelling texts, and consumable workbooks and use the funds saved for purchasing quality literature selections.

2. *Parent Organizations:* Encourage parent associations to raise funds for books.

3. *Book Fairs:* Another way to obtain new books inexpensively is to sponsor book fairs from companies that provide books based on the amount of sales.

4. *Libraries:* Teachers also collect good literature for their classrooms by borrowing books from school and public libraries.

5. *Used Books:* Used books are often of good quality as well. They can be obtained from public libraries at their yearly sales when they weed out older books in order to make room for new selections.

6. *Garage Sales:* Teachers who are familiar with good authors sometimes find quality children's literature at garage sales and used book stores.

7. *Quality Selections:* Refer to Appendix D and in the Bibliography for lists of quality selections. Also, ask other teachers and librarians for recommendations.

Informing Parents About How to Obtain Quality Literature Selections

Parent Letter 12 provides parents with strategies for obtaining good literature.

HOME LEARNING KITS

Many teachers develop learning kits that children sign out and take home so that parents can promote literacy. Most of the activities outlined in this book can be used in learning kits. They include topics such as how to read aloud to children; alternative ways to respond to books; reading predictable literature to develop comprehension; drawing attention to print; how to develop complex thinking; procedures to conduct theme studies and author studies; conducting dictated story sessions; how to focus attention on sentences and phrases; and developing knowledge of words, letters, and sound/symbol relationships.

Components of Home Learning Kits

• *Kits:* Many elementary teachers I know prepare learning kits by placing activities for parents in zip-lock or cloth-made bags.

• *Activities:* Activities appropriate for learning kits are already prepared in the Letters to Parents. Adapt them for the learning kits.

• *Literature:* When activities require literature, include one or two selections into the learning kits as well.

• *Responding to literature:* For kits with literature selections, include numerous ways to respond to books (see Parent Letter 14).

• *Benchmark behaviors:* Parents appreciate teachers including benchmarks of learning behaviors in kits so they can assess how their children are progressing. Refer to Parent Letters 2, 3, 4, and 5.

• *Sign-out cards:* Attach library cards on the outside of the learning kits so children can sign out the cards themselves.

• *Due dates:* Be careful to state a *return date* on each kit. Children sign out these book bags for up to a week at a time.

• *Levels of kits:* Since learning kits are designed for various levels of abilities, teachers make decisions regarding which kits are sent home with particular children depending on their level of development.

• *Response sheets:* Each kit has a response sheet on which parents write the name of their child and the date they signed out the learning kit. Both parents and children are encouraged to make comments about the activity and what they learned from the experience.

• *Lost kits:* Some teachers are concerned when families don't return kits, especially when teachers themselves have purchased the literature selections included in them. One solution to this problem is to organize older reading buddies or parent volunteers who can read to the children at recess or lunch hour. This will ensure that learning kits remain at school.

• *Experience with activities:* Most teachers use strategies outlined in this book before sending comparable strategies home in learning kits. As well, for activities involving literature, it's important that selected books are familiar to the children.

Reading Kit Response Sheet

Name of Child _____   Date _____

Dear Parents and Care-givers:

Please write any comments you have regarding this activity before you return the kit to school.

1. How did your child enjoy this activity?

2. What did you learn about your child during this activity?

3. What questions do you have about this activity?

In this chapter I discussed how classrooms can be organized to promote literacy. In Chapter Three I will outline specific strategies to develop literacy with Emergent and Beginning readers.

Supporting Emergent
and Beginning Readers

In this chapter are numerous practical activities that support reading development for children in the Emergent and Beginning phases of reading. These activities include positive ways to promote literacy in the classroom, ways to respond to literature, reading aloud sessions, conducting dictated stories, and the shared reading process.

POSITIVE PRACTICES FOR PROMOTING READING

As teachers, you are already doing many things in your classrooms that help young children become literate. Following are specific strategies many teachers employ to develop literacy.

Read to Children

Read to your children every day because we know it is one of the most important activities to develop literacy. Read lots of different kinds and forms of books such as predictable pattern literature, poetry, picture books, folk tales, fantasy, and informational books.

The rhyme and rhythm in poetry, songs, and nursery rhymes are particularly enjoyed by the younger children who love to dance to the tunes, sing the songs, and recite the pieces. My granddaughter, Amy, at two and a half years old, sings most of the songs she hears on audiotapes and those she hears on her favorite television shows. After hearing a song a few times, Amy sings along and frequently makes up her own lyrics. At nursery school recently, she learned the song, "Frere Jacques" and was soon using the same tune to sing her own rendition, "Momma's coming, Momma's coming. Home soon, home soon. Here she comes, Here she comes. Up the drive, Up the drive."

Young children also enjoy hearing predictable literature, books with lots of bright illustrations, few lines of print on each page, repeated lines, strong rhythm and rhyme. Books like *Rooster's Off to See the World* by Eric Carle (1999) and *Bear on a Bike* by Stella Blackstone (2000) are good examples of predictable literature. Also choose books that have refrains such as *The Very Quiet Cricket* by Eric Carle (1990) or *The Three Little Pigs* by Edda Reinl (1983). Choose books that relate to young children's experiences like being afraid of the dark, a new baby in the family, or going to the zoo. Make children aware of print in the school and classroom environment by reading aloud signs around the classroom and school to identify the library, principal's office, the washrooms, and notice boards.

Visit Libraries   Take the children to both school and public libraries several times a month so they can look at and choose books themselves. Ask librarians to draw particular attention to books of songs, poetry, predictable books, and those with refrains.

Play Audiotapes   Encourage children to select favorite books to read aloud again and again. Audiotape favorite selections and place them at the listening center where children can listen to familiar stories over and over.

Reading Aloud Strategies   When you read aloud, examine covers of books and make children aware of titles, authors, illustrators, and dedications. Also encourage children to brainstorm about what stories might be about from the pictures on the cover. As you read, hold books so children can see the pictures and print and encourage talk about what's happening on each page. Occasionally invite the children to turn pages so they learn the direction that the pages move through stories. Encourage children to join in reading whenever they can, especially the repeated lines and refrains. This helps them become aware of print. Finally, talk about the things characters did and events that happened in the book.

Encourage Independent Reading   Set up a reading corner in the classroom where you place comfy cushions, stuffed animals, and lots of familiar predictable pattern literature, refrain books, and complex picture books where children can look at and read books. Encourage children to "read" and retell favorite stories to stuffed animals, reading buddies, and friends. Young children thrive on praise, so lavish lots when they attempt to "read" the texts along with you or alone.

Model Independent Reading   Read yourself and ensure that the children see you reading for pleasure. This tells them that you too value reading as a pleasurable activity.

Informing Parents About Practices to Promote Literacy

See Parent Letter 13, which outlines specific practices for parents to engage in to support literacy at home.

WAYS TO RESPOND TO LITERATURE

Children's understanding is extended when they respond to books in a number of ways: when they contemplate questions, talk about books, draw pictures, and dramatize events in stories. Following are some specific ways children can respond to literature. Invite children to participate in *one* of the following activities after books have been read to them:

Illustrations   Invite children to talk about the illustrations or use illustrations to guide them in retelling stories.

Book Talks   Invite two children to tell each other about a book they enjoyed having read to them.

Art   Invite children to draw (paint, cut, and paste) pictures of *one* of the following: a character they liked, an interesting event, a scary part, or funny part.

• Have children make puppets of characters from old socks, paper plates, or paper bags;

• Invite children to make characters in stories from plasticine, clay, or play dough.

Dramatize   Invite children to dramatize stories by acting out episodes.

- Have children retell stories in their own words.

- Invite two children to role play characters in stories.

- Have children role play with a partner and pretend to interview the author about what they liked about their book.

Characters   Ask children to talk about characters they liked best.

Events   Ask children to name things that happened in stories.

Dictation   Invite children to dictate letters to authors telling what they liked about their stories.

- *Composing:* Invite children to dictate different endings, or sequels to stories.

Mapping   Invite children to draw story maps by illustrating events in order as they happened in the story.

Questions   Ask one or two questions after the reading such as: What did you like best about this book? What did you learn from this book?

 ### Informing Parents About Ways to Respond to Literature

Parent Letter 14 describes ways parents can encourage children to respond to literature in order to develop comprehension and understanding of stories.

READING ALOUD

Benefits of Reading Aloud

Reading aloud to young children is probably the most important activity teachers can do to support children's learning. Reading aloud develops oral language, reading concepts, and builds the foundation for writing and spelling. Studies have shown that reading aloud begins at birth, although some experts suggest that babies in the womb also respond positively to music and to the sound of their mother's voice while reading to them. Perhaps it is the rhythm in the music and stories that seem to affect them.

Reading Aloud and Oral Language Development

It is well known that reading aloud fosters oral language development. At six months our granddaughter, Amy, responded to pictures in books, and by nine months, made sounds of animals in the picture books we read to her. At twenty months, she named characters and repeated refrains she heard in stories. She especially loves songs and poetry and "reads" as we read aloud to her. One of her first recognizable spoken words was "book." She picked up pattern books like *I Went Walking*, by Sue Williams (1989) and backed into us clucking like a chicken, "book, book, book," expecting us to lift her up onto our laps to read to her.

Books, like excursions, songs, and movies, are also great sources for telling and retelling stories. It is no surprise that much of the oral language young children use frequently comes from books we read to them.

Reading Aloud and Reading Development

According to research, listening to stories has long-term effects on developing literacy. In the landmark longitudinal study of children from preschool to fifth grade, Gordon Wells (1986) found that reading to children and discussing stories was the single most important factor associated with children's success in school. Wells maintains that when young children hear stories long before they can read independently

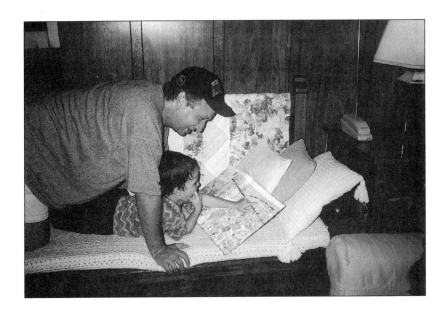

themselves, it helps them understand the organization of written language and its various structures and genres. William Teale (1984) also cites numerous studies that report how storybook reading supports literacy with very young children.

This research informs our family, too, regarding the literacy development of our grandchildren. Our grandson, Nathan, who has been read to since birth, could identify and name all his favorite books by title and author by the age of two. By three, he was "reading" along with his parents, chanting the repeated lines and refrains and by four, he was identifying words in books that were frequently read to him. In fact, one of Nathan's favorite activities is reading books. His friend was really annoyed with him one day when they went to play at his friend's house because all Nathan wanted to do was read books!

Reading aloud develops reading ability in a number of ways. As teachers and parents read aloud, children are invited into new situations; they learn about different characters and how they respond, think, and solve problems. Through factual books, children learn about cars, boats, trucks, castles, dinosaurs, sharks, and other interests they may have. In fact, Gordon Wells (1986) suggests that through reading, children's range of knowledge of the world is extended beyond their immediate experiences.

Children become aware of the function of print during read-aloud sessions. When teachers point to words as they read, children become aware of text, the left to right direction across the page, spaces between words, and the relationship between print and talk.

Reading Aloud and Writing Development

Reading stories to young children supports their writing development in a number of ways. As stories are read to them, children internalize how stories are put together, that stories have characters that do things, that characters usually have problems to solve, and that there are satisfying endings to stories. The language and plots children use in their own compositions often come from the literature that has been read to them. Moreover, drawing attention to text as teachers read contributes to children's awareness of how words are spelled.

Reading and Re-Reading

Children enjoy hearing the same story read over and over again. Although you may get tired of reading the same selection numerous times, children are learning from this activity; they are deepening their understanding, increasing their knowledge of words, exploring new ideas and concepts, discovering the different structures of stories, and are learning the language of books.

Reading Buddies   Since children love hearing the same stories again and again, invite others to read to them as well, such as grandparents, parent volunteers, and older students. Older students in grades four to eight make ideal reading buddies. Arrange with their teachers to come to your classroom once or twice a week to read old favorites to your class. Reading buddies could also re-read children's dictated stories as well.

Read-Aloud Environment

Children benefit from having stories read to them many times a day by both teachers and classroom volunteers. Choose a comfortable place to read to the children: sit in a big chair, on the floor surrounded by soft cushions, or on the carpet. Invite the children to sit close so they can see the illustrations and text.

Informing Parents About the Benefits of Reading Aloud

Parent Letter 15 discusses the benefits of reading aloud to young children.

WORDLESS BOOKS TO DEVELOP LITERACY

Wordless books are books that tell a whole story through illustrations. The absence of words allows children to focus their attention on the illustrations rather than words to help them communicate a plausible story.

The illustrations depict the story and its setting, characters, events, problems, and resolution.

Value of Wordless Books

Using wordless books with young children is particularly useful for emergent readers because they can develop their oral story-telling skills to describe the people, places, and actions depicted in the illustrations. Also, reading wordless books gives children the chance to apply their knowledge of story structures they have learned while listening to stories during read-aloud sessions.

Whole Class Retelling

Introduce children to wordless books by having the whole class get involved in telling a plausible story to correspond with the pictures. Start with a wordless book that has interesting illustrations such as *The Bear and the Fly* by Paula Winter (1976) and do some of the following activities, although these same activities can be used with any wordless book.

Cover   Examine the cover of the story and name the title and author as you frame each word by placing your index fingers on either side of the words.

Oral Story   Invite the children to suggest what might be happening on the cover page. Let them know that you value their ideas by accepting all their suggestions. Continue to examine each picture and illicit story lines for each page. Sometimes you may need to ask a few leading questions to help children think of ideas. But be cautious about asking questions to direct their thinking toward what *you* think would make a good story. Instead, ask gentle, probing questions that cause the children to come up with their own ideas (What do you think is happening on this page? What problems is Father Bear having? What do you think Mother Bear said when Father Bear hit her with the fly swatter? How is Father Bear solving the problems?). Questions like this help children keep control of the composition. Encourage the children to make their characters talk as they create their stories in order to make the characters seem real.

Dictated Chart Story   Look at the wordless book *The Bear and the Fly* again and create a revised story that you copy down onto a chart just as the children tell it.

• *Read the story:* Once the story has been written down on the chart, invite the class to read the story together.

• *Drama:* As a follow-up activity, invite small groups of children to act out the story.

Wordless Books and Personal Dictated Stories

Display numerous wordless books at the Dictation Center and invite children to make up stories to correspond to the pictures while an adult records the story. Some of our favorite wordless books are *Moonlight* by Jan Ormerod (1983), which tells through illustrations about a little girl getting ready for bed. *Overnight Adventure* by Frances Kilbourne (1977) is another favorite because the illustrations in this book suggest real and imagined happenings while camping out in the back yard. Other wordless books are listed in Appendix D.

Storytelling   Invite children to tell their story to a friend, their group, or the class as they turn the pages of the book, showing their classmates the illustrations.

Audiotape   Some children may enjoy telling their stories into an audiotape that can be placed in the Listening Center for others to use.

READING ALOUD PREDICTABLE PATTERN LITERATURE FOR ENJOYMENT

Reading aloud for the shear pleasure of books themselves is a valuable experience that develops literacy. When we read to our grandchildren, we find the whole experience gratifying—we enjoy the book itself and take pleasure in watching our grandchildren's reactions to it. When we first began reading to them as babies, we did most of the responding rather than them. We told them what we liked about the stories and sometimes we would make sound effects for vehicles or sounds that animals make as we read. For example, when we read *Freight Train* by Donald Crews (1978), we made train sounds like, *"chicka, chicka, chicka, chicka, hoo, hoo"* after each line of text. When stories featured different animals as in the story *Let's Go Visiting* by Sue Williams (1998), we made sound effects for the various animals (*"neigh, neigh"* for the foal, *"baa, baa"* for the calves, *"meow, meow"* for the kittens). Very soon, they began to react to the stories too, by making the sounds along with us as we re-read the stories. Occasionally, we'd ask them to point to animals in pictures and encourage them to make an appropriate sound to correspond with each animal. Even though she wasn't yet speaking, Amy, at nine months, would make the sound effects for the various animals in *Brown Bear, Brown Bear, What Do You See?* by Bill Martin Jr. (1992). But when she came to the picture

of the goldfish, she pursed her lips and made a sucking sound that her Dad had shown her, making us all laugh! Our delight encouraged her to do it all the time whenever we'd say, "What does a goldfish say, Amy?" We all thought it was hilarious. The point is that reading aloud to young children without inundating them with questions and follow-up activities is a good thing to do for preschoolers and school-age children alike.

While reading aloud for enjoyment is a relatively natural activity for parents, grandparents, and preschool educators, reading aloud for enjoyment is sometimes difficult for teachers in primary grades because they often feel guilty about spending so much time reading aloud. Even principals and superintendents are not always encouraging of the practice. So, when administrators question why you read aloud so much to your children, remind them that research supports reading aloud to early years children because of the enormous academic benefits it provides them throughout their school lives (Teale, 1984; Wells, 1986). Point out, as well, that numerous studies indicate that learning disabled readers also benefit from having books read aloud to them (Tunnell and Jacobs, 1989).

How to Read Aloud for Enjoyment

Reading aloud for enjoyment is not difficult to do once we know why we're doing it.

Book Selection   Choose interesting books that young children enjoy. Many good selections are listed in Appendix D. Read all kinds of material

like poetry, pattern stories, refrain books, picture books, and information books. At first, read only the books you really like and then watch for books that interest the children and find selections to correspond.

A favorite book of our grandchildren's is *Incy-Wincy Spider* by Katie George (1995). Nathan especially likes this story because the first part follows the traditional action song so there's lots of rhythm and rhyme. But then "Incy" tries to find a safer place to live and looks in all kinds of places. Children have to lift the flaps to investigate until "Incy" finds just the right spot to spin his web. There's even a finger puppet spider to go on the adventure too! After reading this book, Nathan and I made a spider book based on all the places spiders spin their webs at our house on the lake.

Modeling Selection

I chose *Incy-Wincy Spider* by Katie George (1995) for this strategy, although many other books will also work.

Reading the Cover   As you read the cover, point to the title, the author's name, and the name of the illustrator. In this case, Katie George is both author and illustrator. Talk about other books about spiders such as *The Very Busy Spider* (Eric Carle, 1984). Then discuss the picture on the cover.

Reading the Story   Read the story showing your interest and delight in it. Make actions for the spider climbing up the water spout, for the rain falling, and for the sun coming out. Then use sound effects for the water "swooshing" out. Also take on voices for various characters if you have a flair for the dramatic.

Responding to the Book   Just talk about the book: talk about the pictures, about experiences the book reminds you of; talk about how this book connects to other books you have read; talk about parts you loved and language that delighted you. This talk follows no pre-planned structure, and no prescribed curriculum. It is spontaneous talk stimulated by the literature and the natural responses to it that children and teachers make.

Informing Parents About Reading Aloud for Enjoyment

Invite parents to read books for enjoyment. See Parent Letter 16.

READING ALOUD PREDICTABLE PATTERN LITERATURE TO DEVELOP COMPREHENSION

Reading predictable pattern literature to young children not only develops their oral language and reading and writing development, it also promotes understanding and comprehension.

Selections

Several different types of predictable literature work effectively to promote comprehension and understanding. Look for selections that have repeated lines, cumulative sequences, sequential patterns, and rhyme (see Appendix D for suggested titles).

Model Selection   Young children love the story *Just for You* by Mercer Mayer (1975) because it has so many predictable features such as bright pictures, large print, few lines of text per page, repeated sentences, phrases, and words as well as a strong rhythm. Other predictable texts can also be used with the following procedure for future read-aloud sessions.

Reading Covers   Start the read-aloud session by reading the cover of the book and drawing attention to the title, author, and illustrator and talk about what each does (authors write books and illustrators draw or paint the pictures). In this book, Mercer Mayer was both author and illustrator. During successive readings, ask the children to name the title and author/ illustrator themselves. Have a discussion about other books Mercer Mayer has written and start a display of his books.

Building Comprehension   Understanding is developed in a variety of ways:

• *Prediction:* Comprehension begins by examining the cover and think- ing about what might happen in the story. Welcome the children's re- sponses and accept them even though they may be different from yours or the author's, for that matter. Probe gently when you are unclear about the meaning of their responses, by asking "Help me understand why you think that." This shows the children that you have confidence in their ideas. Questions like this also help children clarify their thoughts.

Reading the Story   Read the story to the children with enthusiasm, and invite them to join in with the repeated phrases "I wanted to" and "just for you." Give the children ample opportunity to examine and com- ment on the pictures and story. You can tell if children are connecting to the story when they make spontaneous comments about pictures or events ("Look, she's holding her nose"; "He didn't eat his crusts, I did that too, right?"). Encourage this.

Reading and Re-Reading   Children never seem to get tired of hearing the same story read over and over again, so be prepared to read certain se- lections many times. In each successive reading children gain more and more information about the content, they begin to notice logical cause and effect situations and details in the story. In order to provide additional opportunities to hear the story, audiotape yourself reading during the read-aloud sessions and place these audiocassettes at the Listening Cen- ter so children can listen to the story and follow along with the text and pictures.

Comprehension After Reading

Once you have read the story, have a whole class discussion and then in- vite the children to participate in an independent activity.

Whole Class Discussion   Have a whole class discussion about the book by asking, "How are the experiences of 'Little Critter' like things that have happened to you?" Encourage spontaneous comments and reactions and then ask another question, "What are some problems 'Little Critter' had?"

Independent Activities   Children extend their understanding of predictable pattern literature when they participate in art, drama, and writing activities. (See the section *Learning Activities for Centers* in Chapter Two and *Ways to Respond to Literature* in this chapter.) Young children gain a great deal of satisfaction when they express their ideas through art. Have children choose *one* of the following art activities; after reading another book have them respond through drama and writing activities.

• Children demonstrate their understanding of stories when they draw, paint, and construct pictures of characters, events, and favorite parts of stories. These activities work well for most predictable pattern selections as well as the story *Just for You*.

• Invite children to draw some things Little Critter tried to do.

• Draw a favorite part with crayons.

• Draw a character you liked.

• Draw some events in the story.

• Paint a favorite character, or event from the story.

Comprehension Ideas

Further comprehension ideas (art, drama, and writing) are included in the section *Learning Activities for Centers* in Chapter Two and *Ways to Respond to Literature* in this chapter.

Strategies for Other Predictable Texts

Children need many opportunities to hear predictable pattern stories read to them. The above strategy works well for other predictable pattern selections like sequential pattern selections *The Cat on the Mat* by Brian Wildsmith (1982); cumulative pattern selections *Today Is Monday* by Eric Carle (1993); and rhyming books *Bugs for Lunch* by Facklam (1999).

 ## Informing Parents About Read-Aloud Strategies for Developing Comprehension

See Parent Letter 17, which informs parents about the importance of reading predictable literature aloud to children. This letter may be copied and sent home to parents.

HOW TO CONDUCT READ-ALOUD SESSIONS WITH PREDICTABLE PATTERN LITERATURE TO DEVELOP AWARENESS OF PRINT

Reading predictable pattern literature to children helps them become aware of many concepts of print such as the left to right direction of text across a page, direction pages are turned, spaces between words, and awareness of words.

Selections

Choose predictable pattern literature with repeated lines, cumulative sequences, sequential patterns, and selections that rhyme. (See Appendix D for specific selections.)

Model Selection   We have selected the book *Five Little Monkeys Jumping on the Bed* by Eileen Christelow (1989) as a model for this strategy.

Reading Covers   Start the read-aloud session by asking children to find the title, name of the author, and illustrator. In this selection, the story is retold and illustrated by Eileen Christelow. Make the children aware of print by running your finger under the text as you read this information. Draw attention to specific words on the cover by framing the text as you read the title, author, and illustrator by putting your index finger of each hand at the beginning and end of each word. During another reading ask the children to name the title, author, and illustrator themselves. Next, have a discussion about what authors and illustrators do and talk about other books this author has written.

Reading the Story   Use lots of expression when you read the book, making actions and sound effects whenever possible (scrubbing motions for washing, motions to indicate brushing your teeth, and bouncing motions for the part, "No more jumping on the bed"). Point to the words as you go in order to make children aware of the print and the left to right direction it moves across the page. Stop periodically to allow children time to examine pictures and comment on what's happening. Also encourage children to join in spontaneously with the "reading" of the repeated sentences, phrases, words, and refrains ("Five Little Monkeys jumped on the bed; One fell off and bumped his head.")

• *Re-reading the story:* When you re-read the story, draw specific attention to the repeated text by sweeping your finger under each word as you read. During a third reading consider using a cloze procedure by reading a portion of the predictable pattern and fade out on particular words and have the children read them alone. These procedures help children focus on individual words. Several re-readings also help children become more aware of the left to right and top to bottom direction of print on a page, how pages are turned, and how stories are read.

Attention to Print   Help children focus on print by inviting them to read, copy over, and copy under the predictable sentences in the story.

• *Word pointing:* Print repeated sentences, phrases, and refrains found in the literature in large print onto strips of paper (6 × 18 inches) and have children read the sentence and attempt to point to each word ("One fell off and bumped his head").

• *Over-Copying:* Next, invite children to copy over your print with crayon or markers.

Five little monkeys jumped on the bed.

• *Under-copying:* Print repeated sentences and phrases onto large strips of paper and have children copy under your print.

One fell off and bumped his head.
One fell off and bumped his head

Print Awareness Activities   Several activities help children attend to print.

• *Sentence strips:* Have children practice reading their old sentence strips with a friend while they point to individual words.

• *Chart stories:* Have children work in partners to re-read old chart stories, pointing to each word with a wooden pointer.

• *Tracking print:* Reprint whole texts of stories onto overhead acetates, place them onto an overhead projector in the reading corner, and invite children to "read" stories while pointing to the words.

• *Additional activities:* Also refer to the many interpretive activities described in Chapter Two *Learning Activities for Centers* and *Ways to Respond to Literature* in Chapter Three.

Strategies for Other Predictable Pattern Stories   In order for children to develop firm concepts of print, they will need many experiences with predictable pattern literature. Use the previous strategy for books with repeated lines (*I Can Roar* by Frank Asch, 1985), for cumulative pattern books (*Ten Go Hopping* by Viv Albright, 1985), for sequential patterns (*One Bright Monday Morning* by Arleen and Joseph Baum, 1973), and for rhyming books (*Snuggle Wuggle* by Jonathan London, 2000).

Informing Parents About Reading Pattern Literature to Focus on Print

Parent Letter 18 shows parents how to do this. This letter may be copied and sent home with the children.

REFRAIN BOOKS FOR READING ALOUD TO DEVELOP GENERAL COMPREHENSION: TYPE ONE

Easy-Read Refrain Books

Refrain books are more advanced than predictable pattern literature because the text is more dense and there is more interaction between the characters, events, and problems compared to predictable literature. But like predictable pattern literature, refrain books usually have repeated refrains throughout the story. There are two types of refrain books, easy-read refrain books and traditional refrain books. Easy-read refrain books have moderately dense text and vivid illustrations to accompany each page of print and some interaction between characters, events, and problems. These refrain books have repeated refrains throughout the story. Selections in this category are, *Hattie and the Fox* by Mem Fox (1992); *Mortimer* by Robert Munsch (1985); and *Caps for Sale* by Esphyr Slobodkina (1968).

Traditional refrain books, a second category of refrain book, have more print per page and fewer illustrations than easy-read refrain books described earlier. However, the predictable refrain in these books is easily remembered because of its strong rhythm and repeated lines. Traditional refrain books include: *The Little Red Hen*, *The Three Billy Goats Gruff*, and *The Three Bears* in Tomie de Paola's *Favorite Nursery Tales* (1986). These traditional refrain books have common characteristics: the characters are usually animals; characters usually come in sets of threes (three pigs, three bears, three billy goats); characters are mainly really good or really bad (wolf, troll); there are usually three episodes; and the refrain is repeated over and over.

Although many early years children cannot read refrain books independently, they do understand the concepts in refrain stories at their listening level. In other words, they can listen and understand more complex material that is read to them than they can understand when reading the same material independently.

Model Selection   Easy-read refrain book type one, *Mmm, Cookies* by Robert Munsch (2000), is the selection we'll use for this strategy. This type of refrain book has a moderate amount of print, many illustrations, and a repeated refrain.

Reading the Cover   Start the read-aloud session by reading the cover of the book. Invite children to identify the title, author, and illustrator, providing assistance only when children have difficulty. Then ask children to describe the role of authors and illustrators and have a discussion about other books this author has written.

Building Comprehension Before Reading

After the children have examined the cover illustration, ask them what they think will happen in the story and how it might end. Show them that you value their ideas by responding positively to their responses, even though they might be different from the author's. In this story, for example, children may suspect the story is going to be about a giant bun, because of the cover illustration. If children suggest this notion, explain that this idea could be the basis for a new story, "The Adventures of the Giant Bun." Thus, predictions can never be wrong, they are simply possibilities for new stories.

Reading the Story   Read the story with lots of excitement by changing your voice and pace of reading to represent different characters, events, and moods of the story. Making actions for the different lines in the refrain will be a strong motivator for children to join in with the reading. Invite the children to make up actions to go with each line (*"whap, whap, whap . . . , make it nice and round; swish, swish, swish, sprinkled it with sugar; click, click, click, covered it with yellow icing. . . ."*).

Building Comprehension by Discussing Illustrations

During the reading, examine the pictures and allow children to comment on them informally. Frequently, children demonstrate their understanding of stories by relating events to experiences they have had ("Look, he's throwing the play dough in the air and his mom is going to be really mad because he's making a big mess"). It's important to encourage these spontaneous responses to literature selections.

• *Discussion questions:* Another way to promote understanding of stories is to discuss events in the text. Consider asking questions like, "What's happening here?" "Has anything like this ever happened to you?" "What are the funniest parts?" "What does this story remind you of?" Questions like this are likely to get the children talking. Notice, too, that these questions do not lead to right and wrong answers as those frequently found in commercial reading programs.

Interpretive Activities   Interpreting stories through art, drama, and writing helps children reflect on the story and develop deeper understandings of story elements such as how characters behave, events that happen, problems characters encounter, and ways problems are solved. They do this by engaging in art, drama, and writing activities. Examples of these activities are listed in *Learning Activities for Centers* in Chapter Two. Following are several complex art activities involving construction, puppet making, and modeling.

• *Art:* Encourage children to interpret stories by constructing and modeling characters, events, and problems in them.

• *Modeling:* With play dough, make a character or interesting object in the story (for example, in the story *Mmmm Cookies*, make something you like to eat);

• *Cut and paste:* With colored construction paper and tissue paper make a portrait of a character from the story;

• *Mobile:* Cut out characters from the story using construction paper and attach them with string to a coat hanger.

• *Flannel board:* Make a scene from the story using construction paper and tissue paper and arrange the scene on the flannel board.

• *Puppets:* Make a puppet of one of the characters from paper plates, paper bags, or socks. Decorate the puppet with wool, felt, and buttons.

Comprehension Activities   For additional comprehension activities, refer to *Learning Activities for Centers* found in Chapter Two and *Ways to Respond to Literature*, earlier in this chapter.

Informing Parents About Reading Aloud Easy-Read Refrain Books, to Develop Comprehension

See Parent Letter 19.

TRADITIONAL REFRAIN BOOKS FOR READING ALOUD TO DEVELOP COMPLEX THINKING

This activity is planned for traditional refrain books such as *The Three Little Pigs*, *The Three Bears*, and *The Three Billy Goats Gruff* from Tomie de Paola's *Favorite Nursery Tales* (1986).

Selections

Although this procedure works well for any of the traditional refrain books, we have chosen the story *The Three Billy Goats Gruff* as a model to demonstrate the following activities. Select other refrain books for additional read-aloud sessions.

Reading the Cover   Start the read-aloud session by reading the cover of the book and asking the children to name the title, author, and illustrator, and identify what each does. Talk about other refrain books with which the children are familiar and make a display of them.

Building Comprehension Before Reading

• *Examining covers:* Examine the cover of the book and ask the children, "What do you think the illustrator wants readers to think the story might be about?" "What do you think might happen in the story?" "What kind of story do you think this is (fantasy, factual, realistic)? Explain how you know." Accept the children's responses unconditionally and ask probing questions when you don't fully understand their reasoning.

• *Focus question:* Ask a broad question for children to focus on while they are listening to the story. Choose questions that will initiate discussion rather that questions leading to 'right' and 'wrong' answers. Consider *one* of the following focus questions:

• *Problems:* Listen for problems and think how they relate to other stories you have heard;

• *Events:* Listen for events and think about whether they make sense;

• *Characters:* Think about the characters and ways they were important to the story;

• *Endings:* Think about the ending and other ways the story might have ended;

• *Structure:* Think about how refrain books are structured.

Reading the Story   Read the story with lots of gusto and modulate your voice and pace of reading to represent different characters (troll and billy goats), events, and the setting of the story. Have the children suggest sound effects to use during different parts of the story. Possibilities include clapping hands to represent the "trip trapping" over the bridge; a "roar" when the troll's name is mentioned, and so on. Invite the children to "read" the refrain along with you. Other times, read the story fluently without interruption to allow the children to concentrate on the focus question. Avoid asking questions during this reading.

Comprehension After Reading   After the reading, ask the focus question again ("Let's talk about the structure of the story"). Discuss the structure of *The Three Billy Goats Gruff* and what they noticed about it (refrains, three episodes, sets of three characters, good and bad characters). Write these ideas onto a chart and keep adding new information as children discover new features of refrain books during future read-aloud sessions with other traditional refrain books.

Interpretive Activities   Children develop deeper understandings of stories when they interpret them through art, drama, and writing (see *Learning Activities for Centers* in Chapter Two). Drama is one of the best ways to determine whether children understand stories. While children are participating in drama activities, you have the opportunity to witness the children's understanding of the characters and the events. Following are several drama activities in which young children are able to participate:

• Have children dramatize events, problems, and solutions in stories that have been read to them.

• Role play two characters in the story (Troll and Billy Goat);

• Have a telephone conversation with the Troll;

• Act out the story with friends;

• Act out a scene from the story without talking;

• Make motions of a character and have other children in the group guess who you are;

• Make puppets and have a puppet play of the story.

Strategies for Other Traditional Refrain Books   Follow the previous activities for reading many different traditional refrain books to the children so they will gain more knowledge about how characters, problems, and events work in refrain books. Traditional refrain selections suitable for these activities are listed in Appendix D.

Informing Parents About Traditional Refrain Books

Refer to Parent Letter 20.

COMPLEX PICTURE BOOKS FOR READING ALOUD TO DEVELOP COMPLEX THINKING

Although any book with pictures can rightly be called a picture book (wordless books, predictable pattern selections, refrain books), complex picture books have more dense print compared to predictable pattern selections and refrain books and they generally have no refrains. The text in complex picture books usually covers an entire page; there are fewer illustrations than in refrain books and the story line is more complex portraying fantasy or realistic situations that relate to young children's experiences. Complex picture book selections are usually at children's listening level of comprehension. As they listen to stories, they gain understanding as if they read the same selections themselves.

There are many benefits to your children from reading complex picture books. Children's oral language vocabulary, understanding of information, story structures, and concepts of the world around them is extended through listening to complex picture books. Reading literature at children's listening comprehension level also introduces them to a variety of different literary forms (fantasy, folktales, realistic fiction, and informational material). Children also become aware of the relationships between story elements (characters, settings, problems, solutions), which build strong foundations for composing their own stories.

Teachers lead read-aloud sessions with complex picture books because the text is usually too difficult for young children to read independently. While the teacher reads aloud, children are free to concentrate on the content of the story. As well, when teachers read the story, they model how stories should be read.

Selections

Young children love listening to complex picture books. Preschoolers and early primary children enjoy the *Franklin* series by Paulette Bourgeois. They also delight in the hilarious escapades of characters in books by Robert Munsch. Also look for selections by Brian Wildsmith, Mercer Mayer, and Arnold Lobel.

Model Selection   We have chosen the book *The Owl and the Woodpecker* by Brian Wildsmith (1993) to model this read-aloud strategy.

Reading Covers   Start the read-aloud session by examining the cover and have the children read the title and names of the author and illustrator and identify what each does. Point out that Brian Wildsmith wrote the story and painted the pictures. Talk about other books this author has written and ask the children what they notice about this author's style. Start a collection of this author's books.

Building Comprehension   Comprehension is developed in a number of ways.

• *Predicting:* Invite the children to study the cover and make predictions about the story. Listen for ideas about who the characters might be, where the story takes place, what the story may be about, what the problems could be, and how the story might end. Accept the children's responses and try not to be concerned when children's predictions don't match what the author wrote in the book; tell them that their ideas could make an exciting new version. As well, let them know when they have come up with unique ideas that you didn't think about.

• *Focus question for listening:* Another way to promote more complex thinking is to ask the children *one* big question before starting to read and asking the same question after the reading. Providing only *one* question rather than several small questions about each page ensures that the flow of the story is maintained while you read. Remember, though, ask only *one* question! Here are some examples of listening prompts to get you started:

• *Characters:* "As you listen to the story, think about one of the characters, what they are like, and what you know about them."

• *Problems:* "Think about different problems the characters have in the story and notice if they seem real to you."

• *Endings:* "Think about different endings that could work for this story."

• *Interesting language:* "Listen for language that is special and makes you see and hear things."

Remember though, to use only *one* of these prompts during a reading, so you can have a lengthy discussion after the reading. Other prompts could be used during other complex picture book read-aloud sessions.

Reading the Story   Read the complex picture book using lots of expression by changing the tone of your voice, for each character (Owl and Woodpecker) and use sound effects when appropriate ("Whoooo" for Owl and "tappety tap tap" for Woodpecker). Try to avoid asking a lot of little questions during the reading so the children can focus on listening for information pertaining to the *one* big question that you asked prior to the reading.

Comprehension After Reading

• *Discussion of focus question:* Once the story has been read, follow up with the *same* focus question you asked prior to reading and discuss it ("Think about the characters and what you know about them"). Use the children's ideas to make a chart regarding the features of each character—Owl and Woodpecker.

Interpretive Activities Comprehension is developed further when children participate in activities involving art, drama, and writing. The following activities concentrate on interpreting through composing.

- Dictate your version of the story while an adult scribes;

- Dictate or write a new story based on two different animals;

- Dictate or write a postcard to a favorite character;

- Write or dictate a thank-you note to a character in the story;

- Create a recipe for a character in the story; for this story think about what owls and woodpeckers might eat.

- *Response Journals:* For children who are reading and writing, invite them to dictate or write responses to stories. Provide children with prompt questions to stimulate their thinking such as, "What did the story make you think about?" "What did this story remind you of?" "How is this story like others you have read?"

Comprehension Activities For additional comprehension activities, refer to the list of activities, *Learning Activities for Centers* in Chapter Two and *Ways to Respond to Literature* earlier in this chapter.

Complex Picture Book Strategies Repeat this read-aloud strategy many times with different complex picture book selections. A list of complex picture books is found in Appendix D.

 Informing Parents About Reading Complex Picture Books Aloud for Developing Complex Thinking

Refer to Parent Letter 21.

ISSUE BOOKS

Issue books are a type of complex picture book that deal with issues in children's lives, their families, life at school, their community, and society. Issue books sensitively introduce children to ethical and social justice issues such as name calling, bullying, racial prejudice, gender issues, preserving the environment, cruelty to animals, death, homelessness, and poverty.

Like complex picture books, issue books usually have dense print on each page, there are fewer illustrations than in predictable pattern literature, and the story line is frequently complex. For these reasons, issue books are intended to be read to the children. Although the text in issue books is usually too complex for young children to read independently, children are able to understand the concepts at their listening level of comprehension.

Selections   There are more and more books available that deal with issues. Look for the book, *A Father Like That* by Charlotte Zolotow (1971) which examines the many attributes of what an absent father might be like. The book, *Cat Heaven* by Cynthia Rylant (1997) sensitively deals with the issue of the death of a pet. And environmental issues are effectively revealed in the book, *The World That Jack Built* by Ruth Brown (1990).

Model Selection   For these read-aloud activities, I have chosen the book, *Fly Away Home*, by Eve Bunting (1991), a book dealing with the issue of homelessness. Although the activities following are based on this particular issue, the activities presented could be used with books on any issue.

Reading the Cover   Have the children point to the text on the cover that reveals the name of the title, author, and illustrator. Children generally can identify this text because the print on these words is enlarged. Then discuss the author and illustrator, and talk about other books by Eve Bunting.

Building Comprehension   Ask the children to examine the cover and predict where the story takes place, the mood of the characters in the story, and what the problems might be. Listen carefully to the children's responses and accept all their ideas as possibilities for the story.

• *Focus Question:* In order to encourage complex thinking, have the children listen for ideas related to *one* question. Following are examples of some listening prompts: listen for the problems in the story; listen for how the characters are dealing with their problems; as you listen to the story, notice what this story reminds you of or makes you think about; What are some sad things that happen in the story?

Reading the Story   Read the story thoughtfully right through to the end without stopping so children can concentrate on the focus question you asked prior to the reading.

Comprehension After Reading

• Spontaneous Discussion: Sometimes it's a good idea just to listen to the children's spontaneous reactions to the story before dealing with the focus question. Say something like, "So, what did you think?" This kind of question sometimes results in a natural discussion that gets at the heart of the issues in the story. Try not to moralize or introduce your ideas during this discussion; focus instead on what the children think.

• Discussion of the focus question: Next, follow up with a discussion of the focus question (In this story, how did the characters deal with their problems?). Again, listen carefully to the children's responses and try not to introduce your ideas, showing the children you respect their ability to think about complex issues.

Reflective Connections   In her second-grade classroom, Geraldine Van de Kleut encourages her students to reflect on concepts in issue books and helps them make connections to themselves, their world, and other texts. Sometimes she does this through whole class discussions and other times she encourages children to write their reflections in their literature response journals. For this purpose, she posts a chart to guide their written responses: How does this book make you think about you and your life? How does this book make you think about the world around you? What other books does this book remind you of?

• Children's Questions: Often books like this raise lots of questions, so Geraldine devotes part of the literature discussion for the children to ask their questions which she records on a chart. Then she asks the children to review their questions to see whether the text itself answers them; she encourages the children themselves to answer some of the questions and leaves other questions for the children to ponder about or research answers by finding more books in the library on the subject, or by asking other adults about the issue.

Interpretive Activities   Comprehension, reflection, and complex thinking are developed further when children participate in art, drama, and writing activities. Invite your children to try some of these.

• Paint, draw, or model with plasticine one of the characters in the story.

• Dramatize a scene from the story with some friends.

• Write or dictate a letter to one of the characters in the story.

Text Sets   Another way to organize issue books is to group them related to particular themes. Geraldine has a collection of issue books that correspond to themes on issues such as prejudice, loss of friends, family and pets through death, poverty, accepting people for who they are, aging and memories, and the environment. These text sets based on issues are listed in Appendix D.

DICTATED STORIES AND READING DEVELOPMENT

A dictated story is an oral story told by individual children while adults write it down. Thus, teachers attend to the handwriting, spelling, and grammar issues.

Value of Dictated Stories

Dictated stories are useful in a number of ways in order to promote oral language, reading, and writing development of young children.

Oral Language   When children are provided frequent opportunities to tell and dictate stories (once or twice a week), their oral language usually grows dramatically. Through dictation, children experiment with different story structures such as narratives, fantasy, poetry, and informational pieces. As well, they become familiar with story elements of literature (characters, problems, events, and solutions) and frequently use these structures in their dictated stories.

Reading   Dictating stories also contribute to reading ability. Through the process of dictation, children make the connection between speech and reading, as they realize that what they orally compose can be written down and read back. As teachers scribe, children become aware that letters of the alphabet are used by adults to record their stories, that print is read in a left to right direction, and that there are spaces between clumps of print called *words*. Over time, with opportunities to dictate a new story each week, children eventually begin to recognize familiar phrases, sentences, and words as they read their dictated stories themselves with supportive adults.

Writing   Dictated stories build the foundation for story writing. As children tell their stories they are developing composing skills that parallel those required for composing their own stories. Through dictation, children are introduced to grammar and usage as they observe teachers capitalize names and words at the beginning of sentences, and when teachers employ punctuation at the ends of thoughts (periods, exclamation marks, and question marks).

The Dictation Process

There are several things to consider during the dictated story process.

Topics   Topics for dictated stories are generally chosen by children themselves, although you can offer suggestions to stimulate ideas. However, your suggestions should relate to the children's experiences. In order to prompt topics for dictated stories, say something like, "You might like to tell about your pet; What things do you do with your friends? What are things you do with your family? or tell me about your favorite toys." You will likely find that stories are more elaborate, however, when children decide on their own topics.

Illustrations and Dictation   Having children draw pictures of experiences prior to telling stories sometimes helps them focus on their topics. However, telling stories first and illustrating after dictation like real authors do is still another option.

Recording Stories   There are many things to think about as you record dictation:

• *Format for dictated stories:* Some children prefer dictating stories on single pieces of paper and attach them to paintings and sculptures, while others enjoy dictating their stories into booklets with stapled covers. Many teachers like to keep a record of dictated stories over a term and therefore provide children with individual dictation notebooks with several pages in which dictated stories are recorded.

• *Manuscript print (small letters):* We recommend using pencils or markers to record dictated stories using lowercase letters (small letters versus capital letters) and manuscript symbols that are used in commercial print as opposed to cursive writing adults usually employ to write their own correspondence.

• *Speed of recording:* As children talk, begin printing down what is said as quickly as possible. At first, you may find that you can't print as quickly as children speak, so ask them to slow down a bit. Eventually, you will find a pace of recording that matches the speed with which children tell their stories.

• *Record exact speech:* It's also important to record exactly what children say, so avoid changing their language to something more sophisticated. Remember, this is the child's story, not yours.

• *Prompting questions:* During the dictation session, some children require prompts when they run out of things to say about their topics, so ask questions to extend stories to at least five to ten sentences. The following questions usually work well to get children to extend their stories: "So then what happened?" "What happened after that?" "That sounds pretty funny, tell more about that part."

• *Spontaneous dictated stories:* Often, dictated stories are spontaneously motivated by some exciting thing that has just happened. This was the case when I called our five-year-old grandson, Nathan, on the day his baby brother was born. He started to tell me all about it and then I had him stop, and wait till I got a pencil and paper to write everything down. Another time Nathan fell and banged his tooth on the slide. His story about going to the dentist is below.

Reading Dictated Stories   Dictated stories are read in a number of different ways:

• *Adults read to children:* Once the dictated story is complete, you read it back *to* the child while sweeping your index finger under the text as you go.

• *Reading together:* Invite children to read their dictated stories along with you. Fade out when children read certain parts accurately and fade back in when they have difficulty.

• *Reading alone:* Most children at the Emergent and Beginning phase are not able to read their personal dictated stories independently at first, so you need to read their dictated stories to them. Only invite children to read their dictated stories alone when they have begun reading familiar predictable pattern literature with confidence during the Developing and Independent phases.

Dictated Stories and Oral Language Development   Keeping dictated stories over time provide a developmental record of children's oral language growth. This is especially true for children who have immature speech.

I fell on the slide and I crunched my teeth and it started to bleed. I had to go to the dentist. The girl had to see my teeth. The other girl put that little thing in my mouth. She took an Xray. I got off the chair and I took a toy. The dentist said that I can't eat any crunchy stuff because it would hurt my front teeth. After the dentist I went to the store and got a monkey toy. Now I'm feeling a bit better.

Nathan Age 4

• *Immature speech:* When children use immature speech patterns or grammatically inaccurate language in their dictation it's probably best not to read it back to them. Instead, use these immature dictated stories as a record of their oral language development over time. Several strategies improve children's oral language. When children with oral language delays interact with other children and adults who speak standard English, their language usually develops quite naturally. Having children listen to quality literature is another way to expose youngsters to appropriate language structures. This can be accomplished through read-aloud sessions and when children hear good literature at the Listening Center or on video. Some teachers and parents are anxious to correct children's immature speech, but research suggests that over-correcting children's developing speech patterns frequently leads to regressive growth in oral language development. You may want to consult with the school speech therapist for other suggestions for encouraging standard speech.

After Dictation Activities   Once dictation is complete, invite children to participate in some of the following activities:

• Children who enjoy drawing may illustrate their stories using crayons or markers.

• Have children retell their dictated story to a peer, parent volunteer, or reading buddy but don't be surprised when children don't recall all the events in their stories.

• Invite children to work with partners and dramatize an episode from their dictated story.

Frequency of Dictation   Children benefit enormously from the dictated story process, so opportunities to dictate stories two or three times a week is ideal. However, realistically, teachers may only have time to take dictation from individual children once a week or once every two weeks.

Alternative Ways to Take Dictation   Many teachers invite parent volunteers or older reading buddies to take dictation.

• *Parent volunteers and dictation buddies:* Shelley Kropf, a first-grade teacher, provides opportunities for dictating stories once a week for each of her thirty first-grade students. In addition, she trains parent volunteers to assist her. They set up a roster of children's names and simply rotate down the chart on a regular basis so children know when their turn is coming up by observing the chart. Thus, children receive at least one opportunity each week to dictate a personal story.

Dictated Story Sample

Marcus' dictated story below was dictated to his mom while Marcus was in second grade.

Johnny Apple Seed

Once upon a time there was a guy named Johnny. He was pulling apples from an apple tree. Then he saw people coming. They were talking about Johnny. Then he saw something. It was an angel. The angel had a peeled apple in his hand. The angel told him something. And after the angel was talking, he sang Johnny a cool song. Johnny was happy and he decided to go somewhere that did not have any trees at all. Johnny went past the river and past the waterfalls and into the woods. He found a shovel. All the animals were watching what he was doing. The rabbits, a bear and a racoon and a lion was looking at him on a tree. And a skunk came by and he was digging in the ground to see what was under it. And all the skunk found was a seed. When Johnny was looking, the skunk got scared and when Johnny walked towards the skunk, the skunk was going to spray him. But Johnny pet the skunk and the skunk was happy and did not spray Johnny. Johnny pet the racoon too. And Johnny saw some other people making apple pies and other things made from apples. Soon Johnny became

Continued

old and his shadow was bigger than before. Johnny was making apple seeds for the rest of his life. While Johnny was resting the angel appeared again. Then somebody else came out of Johnny and he was old like Johnny. He had a long beard like Johnny. He had the same hair and skin like Johnny. But he didn't have the same voice. It was an angel too. The angel said, "Come on, let's go." But the angel who looked like Johnny noticed something. He noticed a person lying on the grass. "What's that?" said the other angel. "Why that's Johnny," said the angel. The other angel thought, "I can't go. I must stay here with Johnny." The angel told him something and then the other angel felt much better and then the angel said, "Now you want to come." And then they went.

  The End.

Activities for Children Not Dictating Stories   While the teacher is working with individual children recording their dictated stories, the rest of the class participates in activities in various learning centers. The activities at the learning centers are designed to further develop literacy and are both productive and interesting. Plan activities that are accomplished easily by children independently and require no assistance from the teacher. The following learning centers are designed for five to seven children at a time.

• *Reading center:* In the reading center place numerous literature selections, familiar pattern selections, refrain books, complex picture books, and informational books. Also put familiar Big Books the children have made as well as chart stories composed during social studies or science themes.

• *Listening center:* Here, children listen to audiocassettes of literature selections as they follow along with accompanying small books or follow the text in the corresponding Big Book.

- *Painting center:* At the painting center children paint pictures of experiences they have had or illustrate characters and events from literature selections.

- *Puppet center:* Children make puppets of characters in stories they have heard from paper plates, socks, paper bags, and construction paper.

- *Modeling center:* Children create characters with plasticine or clay and objects portrayed in familiar stories.

- *Word study:* Children reinforce their knowledge of words by re-reading familiar sentence strips, match word cards to those on familiar sentence strips, or create new sentences from cut-up word cards.

- *Phonics activities:* Children cut out pictures from magazines that begin or end with designated letter/sound symbols.

- *Other center activities:* For additional center activities, refer to the section *Activities for Learning Centers* found in Chapter Two.

Informing Parents About Dictated Stories

In order to help parents understand about how to conduct dictated story sessions, send home Parent Letter 22, which outlines the procedure.

SMALL GROUP DICTATION

Some teachers work with small groups for dictating stories, which is easier to organize for some teachers. In this procedure individuals dictate complete stories, while the whole group reads them together.

1. *Child dictates:* One child in the group dictates a complete story while the teacher records it onto a chart. The other group members watch and listen.

2. *Group reads:* Once the dictated story is complete, the teacher and group read the dictated story together in unison.

3. *Individual reads:* The child who dictated the story reads the story alone while the teacher provides support when necessary.

4. *Group reads:* The whole group reads the completed dictated story together once more.

5. *Child illustrates:* The child who dictated the story illustrates it.

6. *New story begun:* During the next session, a different child in the group dictates a story and this process continues until every group member has an opportunity to dictate a story.

Dictated Sentences

A dictated sentence is a single thought children dictate while adults record it onto a strip of paper. Dictating sentences is a valuable procedure for developing literacy because it helps children become aware of manageable chunks of text as they learn concepts of print, become familiar with sentences, identify words, and develop handwriting skills.

Recording Sentences   Teachers or adult volunteers record sentences that children dictate onto strips of paper about 6″ × 18″ long.

• *Small letters in manuscript print:* On this strip of paper use a marker to record the dictated sentence in enlarged print using lowercase letters (small letters versus capital letters) and manuscript symbols that are used in commercial print as opposed to cursive writing that adults usually use for their personal writing.

• *Record exact speech:* It's important to record exactly what children say, which shows that you value them as language users. So, avoid changing the language they use to more complex forms.

Topics for Dictated Sentences   Ideas for dictated sentences ideally come from the children themselves, but sometimes ideas for sentences are stimulated by their paintings, drawings, personal experiences, and literature they have heard.

• *Prompts:* Ask questions to prompt sentences, "What's happening in your picture?" "What's one thing you really liked about the story?"

Reading Dictated Sentences   Both adults and children read dictated sentences in a number of ways:

• *Teachers read:* First you read the dictated sentence to the child while sweeping your finger under the text in order to draw attention to each word.

• *Reading in tandem:* Next, you and the child read the dictated sentence together, while you point to each word.

• *Reading alone:* Invite the child to read their sentence alone while you point to each word. As children read, you fade out, but when children have difficulty, you chime back in to give them support.

• *Expectations:* Some children will be able to read the text along with you while others will not, so it is unwise to expect all children at the Emergent phase to read their dictated sentences fluently.

Copying Sentence Strips   Invite children to copy over and under sentences. See examples in figures on page 64.

• *Over-Copying:* Children copy directly over the teacher's print on the sentence strip with crayons or markers in order to develop handwriting ability. Don't be surprised if over-copying is a bit wobbly at first. With time and experience, children's dexterity will improve.

• *Under-Copying:* Notice the development in children's ability to copy over sentences. When over-copying becomes quite controlled, have children copy *under* dictated sentences as well as copying over them. This will further develop their hand writing ability and at the same time makes them aware of words and letters of the alphabet.

Re-Reading   Read sentence strips in a number of ways, by having adults read sentence strips to children, adults and children read the sentence together, and finally, children read the sentence strip alone, while you fade in and out to provide support.

- *Review sentence strips:* Keep sentence strips stored in the children's dictated story booklet or hang them on hooks around the classroom. Every so often, gather up these old familiar sentence strips and have the children re-read them with parent volunteers and reading buddies.

Informing Parents About How to Dictate Family Stories

Parent Letter 23 shows parents how they can dictate family stories in scrapbooks and photograph albums.

Informing Parents About Dictated Sentences

The dictated sentence process is a useful activity for parents to do at home. See Parent Letter 24, which outlines the dictated sentence process for parents.

CHART STORIES

Teachers often invite their class to orally compose stories about classroom activities (making applesauce, baking cookies, special visitors) and out of class experiences (visiting an apple orchard, nursery, pizza parlor).

Whole class chart stories are important in promoting literacy. As teachers record class stories, young children connect their experiences to the printed word. At the same time, these dictated stories composed by the class provide relevant reading material for them. As well, while teachers record stories they model conventional spelling and grammar usage: "We need a capital letter here because it's the name of a person. We put this dot, we call a period, at the end of Ron's sentence to show that he has completed an idea. And we put these quotation marks (" ") to show what Linda said." Many teachers also invite the children to help out occasionally with the spelling and grammar.

Recording Class Chart Stories   Teachers ask their class to think about things that happened such as steps they took to make applesauce or things they saw and did on the excursion to the farm. Children are asked to offer ideas, which teachers record onto chart paper. Usually, children offer single sentences until the chart is full.

Reading Chart Stories   Once chart stories are complete, they are read by both children and teachers in a number of ways:

- *Teachers read:* Teachers read chart stories to the class while pointing to each word;

- *Tandem reading:* Children and teachers read chart stories together;

- *Authors read:* Children who offered sentences read their sentences aloud while attempting to point to each word;

- *Volunteers read:* Children volunteer to read certain sentences. While children read, teachers read along too, fading in and out to maintain fluency while they point to each word in the story.

Samples of Chart Stories   The chart below on how to make applesauce was prompted by a social studies theme on Apples. The children in Wayne Gingrich's class had already visited an apple orchard, had read numerous books about apples, wrote stories about apples, and made apple pie. This chart was dictated by the class outlining the steps involved in making the pie.

Apple Pie

1. Wash your hands.

2. Mrs. Sauder will help to make the pie crust.

3. Peel and slice the apples.

4. Fill the pie shell with sliced apples.

5. Add a little cinnamon and sugar.

6. Bake the pie.

7. Enjoy eating it!

• *Thank-you letters:* Chart stories are also useful for thanking people for sharing special events with them. Mrs. Moore's first-grade class had a great time when a neighborhood farmer brought several farm animals to their classroom. She packed a duck, cats, their dog, rabbits, and a goat into her car and headed off to school! She asked a neighbor, Doug, to come along to help manage the animals. The children had a wonderful time patting the animals and then the goat relieved himself on the floor, which amazed and delighted the children. After the visit the class wrote a thank-you letter to Doug, which is illustrated below.

Janet Lee School

Dear Doug,
   Thank you for bringing the goat. We're glad the goat didn't pooh on our shoes!! Thank you for packing and driving the car.
                    Mrs. Moore's Grade Ones

SHARED READING

The shared reading process is one of the most effective procedures for reading instruction. First introduced by Don Holdaway from New Zealand in the early 1980s, teachers across North America have been conducting shared reading processes for decades. The shared reading process is effective in numerous ways to develop literacy.

Predictable Pattern Literature

Predictable pattern literature is mainly used in the shared reading process because it is easily read due to its unique features such as small amounts of text per page, illustrations that support the text, repeated lines, refrains, strong rhythm, and rhyme. Because of the features of predictable literature (especially few lines of print on each page), children easily learn to read the repeated sentences, phrases, and words. Moreover, they continue to learn how print works—the left to right direction of written language and the left to right movement of pages through books.

Comprehension   The shared reading process develops comprehension because of the numerous activities that children engage in to respond to pattern literature selections. These activities reinforce skills of predicting, sequencing, cause and effect, and knowledge of story elements (characters, setting, events, problems, and solutions).

Reading Strategies   Predictable pattern literature provides a context to learn sentences, phrases, and words. Predictable literature is also a meaningful context for children to employ numerous cueing strategies in concert with one another. These include strategies to help make sense of the story like recalling the story, using pictures, and thinking about what would make sense (semantics), word patterns (syntax), and grapho-phonics (letter/sound relationships).

THE COMPONENTS OF THE SHARED READING PROCESS

The shared reading process has several components involving reading the selection, developing comprehension, focusing on text, making Big Books, assisted reading, building understanding of words, and employing cueing systems. Shared reading activities may continue over several days. Following is the step by step shared reading procedure.

Day One: Introduction of the Story

Selections

Predictable pattern literature is used for the shared reading process because of its many features, which make texts easy to read (minimal print per page, colorful illustrations, repeated lines and refrains, rhyme and rhythm). Many predictable pattern selections work well for the shared reading process such as selections with repeated lines such as *Who Says Moo?* by Ruth Young (1997); books with sequential patterns, *First Flight* by David McPhail (1987); cumulative selections such as *The Napping House* by Audrey Wood (1984); and rhyming selections, *Together*, by George Ella Lyon (1989). For specific literature selections suitable for shared reading activities see Appendix D.

Model Selection   I have chosen *The Chick and the Duckling* by Mirra Ginsberg to model the shared reading process because of the sequential pattern, minimal text per page, quality illustrations, and repeated lines.

Reading Covers   Children learn about the features of books when they examine the title, author, illustrator, and dedication and talk about what each does. This information is useful when children make their own Big Books and write compositions of their own.

Building Comprehension   Ask the children what they already know about chicks and ducklings and develop a chart to record their ideas.

• *Focus question:* Teachers give the children a big question on which to focus their listening while the teacher reads the story: Listen for things characters do in the story; listen for problems in the story (Chicks and Ducklings); think about alternative endings. Since these questions are generic, they can be used for many different selections.

What We Know About Chicks

They lay eggs.

They are an egg when they are first born.
Their mother warms them up to hatch.

What We Know About Ducks

Ducks have webbed feet.

They like the water a lot.

Ducklings can swim a couple of
    hours after they're born.

Read the Selection   Teachers dramatically read the selection to the children and invite them to join in with the predictable parts such as re-peated phrases, sentences, and refrains ("Me too," said the Chick).

- *Re-Read:* Re-read the story in a variety of ways to focus on text.
- *Teachers read:* Teachers read the pattern selection again drawing atten-tion to print by pointing to some key words in the story; in this story, point to the words *Duckling* and *Chick* and ask children to make duck and chick sounds.
- *Teachers read again:* You read the piece again and have the children read the words *Duckling* and *Chick* along with you.
- *Teachers and children read:* Teachers invite the class to join in with the reading of the predictable portions of the text, such as the repeated lines and refrains "'Me too,'" said the Chick."
- *Children read:* Half the class reads the part of the Duckling ("I am going to _____ said the Duckling") and the other half reads the part that the Chick says ("Me too, said the Chick").

After Reading Comprehension

- *Discussion of focus question:* Here, the teacher and children in Mrs. Hedge's Kindergarten class discuss the focus question asked prior to reading the story (What can the characters do?). Teachers add new ideas of the children to the chart regarding what Ducklings can do and what Chicks can do. This information was then transferred to a Venn diagram.

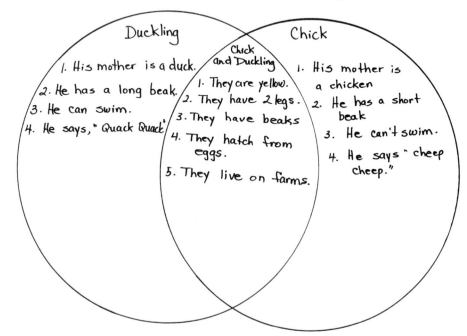

- *Class discussion:* A second discussion develops comprehension further as children discuss *one* aspect of the story such as comparing characters, examining problems, considering solutions, discussing alternative endings, and talking about what they learned from the story.

Interpretive Activities   Children extend their knowledge of stories when they are involved in art, drama, and writing activities. Several center activities are set up for this purpose. See specific center activities at the end of the section on Shared Reading.

Day Two: Making Big Books

In preparation for Day Two, reprint the text from the pattern selection in large print onto long pieces of paper (12 × 18 inches). Write a small amount of text at the top of the paper in order to model that print moves left to right and from top to bottom of pages. The remaining space under the text is reserved for children to illustrate the text.

Reading the Big Book   Teachers and children read the loose pages of the Big Book together while the teacher points to each word.

Illustrating Text   Teachers invite children to illustrate a page of the Big Book alone or with a partner using crayons, paint, or cut and paste materials. This is a wonderful opportunity for children to experiment with alternative art media. Some children are asked to illustrate the cover for the Big Book. Usually there are not a sufficient number of pages in the Big

Book for all children to illustrate, so while some classmates are illustrating, others participate in center activities related to the story such as modeling, drawing, painting, making puppets, copying sentence strips, and the like. See the center activities at the end of this section. For additional ideas, see *Learning Activities for Centers* in Chapter Two.

Assembling the Big Book   Once the illustrations are complete, teachers re-read the original pattern selection to support children in assembling the pages of the Big Book in the appropriate order.

Re-Reading the Big Book   Teachers invite the class to re-read the Big Book in a number of ways while the teacher points to each word on a line of text:

• Teachers read a page and the class make sound effects and actions for a character on each page (Duckling noises and Chick noises);

• Teachers and children read the whole story in unison;

• Teachers read the narration and the class reads the repeated lines and refrains;

• Teachers read one page and then the class alternates reading the next page together;

• Illustrators read their page;

• Children volunteer to read a page independently while the teacher provides support when necessary.

Putting the Big Book Together   Teachers help the children create an authors' page (for example, "This book was illustrated by Janice, Norinder, Vlademeer, Josie, Fredrica"). The class decides to whom they wish to dedicate the Big Book ("This Big Book is dedicated to the Kindergarten class"). The front and back covers are then laminated before stapling the pages of the Big Book together with a heavy duty stapler. Many teachers put book-binding tape over the staples for added strength.

Day Three: Sentence and Word Study

On day three the class focuses specifically on recognizing sentences and words.

Re-Reading Big Books   The class reads and re-reads the Big Book in different ways: in unison, with partners, in two parts, and individuals read the parts they illustrated.

Sentence Strips   Teachers select repeated lines from the story and print them onto sentence strips (6″ × 18″). These sentence strips are posted on charts or blackboards to study as a whole class.

Reading Sentence Strips   Read the sentence strips in different ways:

• The class reads sentence strips in unison while teachers point to individual words;

• Individual children point to words on sentence strips while the class reads them together;

• Teachers point to first and last words in sentence strips and the class reads the words;

• Individual children frame particular words named by the teacher (find the word *Duckling* in this sentence strip);

• Individual children identify words they know on sentence strips by pointing and saying the words.

Center Activities   Children extend their learning by engaging in the various center activities (see the end of this section for specific examples of activities).

Day Four: Sentence Strip Activities for Individuals

Children are provided with several laminated sentence strips with repeated lines from the literature selection. Individual children do one of the following activities:

• *Over-Copying:* Children copy over the teacher's print with washable markers or crayon.

• *Under-Copying:* Children copy under the teacher's text with washable markers or crayons.

Me too, said the Chick.
Me too said the Chick

Word Study   Finally, attention is drawn to individual words within predictable sentences. This is done by:

• *Word pointing:* Children point to individual words as they re-read sentence strips;

• *Framing:* Individual children frame words they know in sentence strips by placing their first finger on their left hand at the beginning of the word and then placing the first finger of their right hand at the end of the word;

• *Word matching:* Teachers make a second sentence strip identical to the first and cut it up for children to match words to the original sentence strip;

- *Sentence creating:* Children use cut-up words to create new sentences;

- *Sorting words:* Children sort words from cut-up sentence strips into categories (things, actions, colors, animals, etc.);

- *Word keys:* Children create word keys by placing words they recognize onto key chains.

Center Activities   Children develop more understanding of the selection when they engage in the various center activities described at the end of this section.

Day Five: Developing Phonic Awareness

Teachers develop phonic awareness by having children examine the Big Book for words that begin and end with particular sound/symbols. First, re-read the Big Book together as a class before participating in some of the following activities.

Names   Names of children in the class are used to develop phonic awareness in the context of familiar Big Books.

- *Beginning sounds:* Children find words in the Big Book that begin like names of various children in the class. The teachers asks, "Who can find words in the story that begin like *Darlene?*" Then, Darlene finds the words *Duckling* and *digging;* Simron finds the words *swimming* and *said.*

- *Ending sounds:* Children find words in the Big Book that end with certain sounds like *t* for instance. The children find the words *out, caught, not.*

Similar Sounds   Children find words in the Big Book that begin with similar sound/symbols (all the words that begin with *s, t, m,* etc.).

- *Ending sounds:* Children find words that end with similar sound/symbols (*d, n, p, t,* etc.).

Rhyming Words   Children think of words that rhyme with words in the Big Book (*shell, bell; out, shout; walk, talk*).

Create Rhyming Families   Children create lists of rhyming words based on words from the Big Book (*dig, fig, big; hole, pole, roll*). Have the children name the letter at the beginning of each new rhyming word.

Day Six: Writing a New Version

Rewrite a new story by using the pattern from the Big Book as a basis for the new version. Children in Mrs. Hedges' kindergarten class used the story *The Chick and the Duckling* as the model for their story about dinosaurs. The children dictated their new story onto a chart before Mrs. Hedges made it into a Big Book. The children then made illustrations from construction paper and had the book laminated and bound. At the end of their story, they included a Venn diagram demonstrating their knowledge of the Brachiosaurus and Stegosaurus.

The Dinosaurs

The dinosaurs hatched out of the eggs.

Brachiosaurus said, " I'm going to take a walk." Stegosaurus said, "Me too!"

Brachiosaurus said, " I'm going to eat some plants." Stegosaurus said, "Me too!"

Brachiosaurus said, "I'm going in the water." Stegosaurus said, "Me too!"

Stegosaurus sank to the bottom.

Brachiosaurus saved him.

Brachiosaurus said," I'm going back into the water." Stegosaurus said, " Not me!"

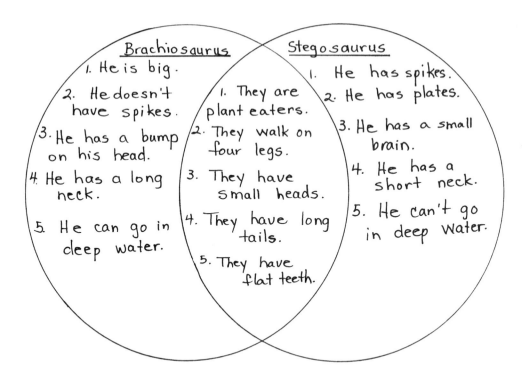

Day Seven: Activity Centers

Teachers set up several activity centers where children consolidate their understanding of the concepts in the Big Book. These learning centers include listening, puppets, drama, painting, modeling, reading corners, sentence strip activities, and writing. Also see additional center activities *Activities for Learning Centers* in Chapter Two.

Listening Center   At the listening center small groups of children listen to an audiotape of one of the predictable pattern selections previously studied and follow along with the text on corresponding Big Books or the original commercial book upon which the Big Book was based. For the story *The Chick and the Duckling,* have the children listen to other stories about chicks and ducks.

Puppet Center   Children make puppets from paper plates, bags, or socks and act out a scene from the Big Book. (For this story, make puppets of chicks and duckings.)

Drama Center   Children use materials from the dress-up box as props to dramatize parts of the story in the Big Book:

- *Charades:* Children act out a character (the Chick or Duckling) from the Big Book and have others guess who the character is;

- *Mime:* Children act out parts of the story from the Big Book using actions only.

Painting Center   Set up a painting station where children paint characters and scenes from the Big Book.

Modeling Center   Children love modeling characters from the Big Book with plasticine, play dough, and clay.

Big Book Center   Children in small groups practice re-reading in unison the Big Book.

- Acetate stories: Teachers re-write the Big Book story onto overhead acetates for children to practice their reading.

Sentence Strip Activities   Children copy over and copy under familiar sentences from the Big Book.

Word Sorting   Children sort words from the Big Book in varieties of ways (according to action words, animals, things, colors, etc.).

Phonics   Children play "I Spy" with one another to identify words from the Big Book that begin with certain sounds and end with particular sounds.

Writing   Children compose stories based on the Big Book in a variety of ways:

- *Dictated stories:* Children dictate their own renditions based on the Big Book.

- *Personal writing:* Children compose and record their own stories using the spelling strategies they know (scribble, random letters, approximate spelling).

This chapter outlined specific activities suitable for Emergent and Beginning readers. Chapter Four describes instructional strategies for Developing and Independent readers.

4

Teaching Developing
and Independent Readers

DEVELOPING RECOGNITION OF PHRASES
AND SENTENCES

There are several strategies that help children pay particular attention to phrases and sentences in the environment. These include dictating sentences, identifying sentences and phrases in literature, and composing sentences based on predictable pattern literature.

Recognizing Phrases and Sentences in the Environment

Much has been written about the value of print in the environment and how it supports early reading. Thus, drawing children's attention to phrases and sentences on signs around the classroom and school is useful to develop literacy. Labeling things around the classroom in sentences or phrases also builds understanding of print. Following are several ways to extend understanding of phrases and sentences in the school environment.

Signs Around the School   Take the children for a walk around the school to look for phrases and sentences on signs. You may notice signs such as, *Visitors Report to the Office, Bus Loading Zone, The Library Is Closed, Wear Sneakers in the Gym*. Also, notice signs around the classroom. Read the sign on the bulletin board, *Art by First Grade, Hang Back Packs Here*, or the chart on the blackboard that says *Our Daily News Chart*.

Label the Classroom   Children become more aware of sentences when you label the learning activity centers such as, *This is the book center; This is the block center; This is the listening center*.

Chart Stories   Composing chart stories is another way children become aware of sentences. Develop dictated story charts based on field trips you have taken with the class. Invite individual children to compose single sentences, and once the chart is complete, read it back together and then have those that contributed sentences read theirs.

Message Box   Write good-news messages to the children telling them how special they are. Invite them to write notes to each other and to you.

Public Service Signs   Invite your class to suggest good habits for children in the classroom and school and post them in strategic places (*Wipe your feet before you come into the classroom; Wash your hands with soap and water; Don't run in the halls; Put a hat on before going outside; Wait in line for your bus*).

Dictated Sentences   The dictated sentence process outlined previously in Chapter Three is an excellent way to help children compose and read sentences and phrases. Copying over and copying under sentence strips gives children additional practice in reading phrases and sentences.

Reading Walls   Read phrases and sentences around the school and classroom to the children on a regular basis and invite them to use a pointer and read the signs themselves.

Informing Parents About Making Children Aware of Phrases and Sentences in the Environment

Help parents understand the importance of making children aware of phrases and sentences in their environment by sending home Parent Letter 25.

Predictable Patterns from Literature

The repeated phrases and sentences in predictable pattern literature are frequently the first lines of print young children recognize.

Repeated Lines   Choose repeated lines from predictable pattern literature to print onto sentence strips. For example, two different sentence strips can be made from sentences in the story *Dear Zoo* by Rod Campbell (1985): *They sent me a _____* and *I sent him back.* A sentence strip can also be made from the repeated sentence in the story *Peace at Last* by Jill Murphy (1982), *"Oh, No!" said Mr. Bear, "I can't stand this"* which is repeated throughout the story.

Activities with Sentence Strips   Read sentence strips in a number of ways to and with children; have them copy over your print and then under your print so they get additional experiences reading phrases and sentences.

Composing New Stories Based on Predictable Pattern Literature

Composing new stories based on predictable pattern literature is a good way to help children recognize phrases and sentences.

Reading Selections   Choose favorite pattern selections already familiar to the class and compose new versions. For example, during a fall theme use the pattern book *Brown Bear, Brown Bear, What Do You See?* by Bill Martin Jr. (1992) as the basis for a new story. Read the story to the class and invite them to join in with the reading of the predictable parts (*"Brown Bear, Brown Bear, What do you see? I see a _____ looking at me"*).

Brainstorm for New Ideas   Brainstorm with your class things they notice about spring (dew drops, buds, birds, flowers, etc.). Then brainstorm for alternative characters for the story (green buds, blue birds, black snakes, brown rabbits).

Compose   Then create a new version related to the original pattern book. Record the children's ideas on a chart.

Big Books   Children gain more practice reading phrases and sentences when you make the new story into a Big Book. Make the Big Book by copying each line onto a separate page (12" × 18") and have children illustrate each page using art media such as crayon, pastels, tissue paper, construction paper, or paint.

• Publishing: Add laminated covers, create author, illustrator, and dedication pages, and bind the Big Book together with heavy duty staples.

Read and Re-Read   Read and re-read the Big Book numerous times so children internalize the phrases and sentences: teachers read the question part and the children read the response, "*I see a* _____"; children read the question and the teacher reads the response; half the class reads the question and the other half read the response; illustrators read their own pages.

Distribute   Share the Big Book publicly by putting it into the reading corner for individual children to enjoy; display the Big Book in the school library along with the literature selection upon which it was based; and send the Big Book home for parents to read to their children.

Informing Parents About Composing New Versions Based on Pattern Literature

Parent Letter 26 outlines how parents can create new versions of pattern literature with their children. Send it home along with two or three pattern books for parents to use as models.

WORD KNOWLEDGE

Most researchers agree that words are learned more effectively when they come from contexts that are meaningful to children such as good literature, dictated sentences, stories, and charts. It also makes good sense to learn words in texts with which children are familiar. However, reading individual words is a complex process that evolves over long periods of time and involves numerous, diverse experiences with print in meaningful contexts. For example, children are naturally introduced to words when they listen to stories being read to them during read-aloud sessions, during the shared reading process, as they dictate sentences, when they over-copy and under-copy sentences, and as they develop captions for their paintings. Although research has shown that some children become aware of words without formal instruction, knowledge of individual words is emphasized by noting words in the school and classroom environment, labeling objects around the school and classroom, by examining captions in literature, dictating and reading dictated sentences, and composing captions for child-composed books.

Developing Knowledge of Words in the School Environment

Children are surrounded by words in their home and school environments. The school is a good place to start helping children become aware of environmental print.

Children's Names   One of the first ways to make children aware of words is to draw attention to their names. Label children's names whenever you can to identify their artwork, writing, and storage bins. Also encourage parents to label their children's clothing, running shoes, mitts, hats, lunch containers, and backpacks. Print names in manuscript print that resembles print found in a book and use lowercase (small) letters rather than capitals.

Environmental Words   Whenever you can, point out words around the classroom such as the names of centers and room number of the classroom. As well, point out words in the school such as the name of the school, names on doors of washrooms, library, principal's office, staff room, supply room, and exits.

Labeling Around the Classroom   Children also enjoy labeling items around the classroom. Involve the children in choosing what is to be labeled while you print the words. Then post the labels on the various objects: door, windows, blackboard, shelves, books, garbage can, desk, and so on. Have children try to find words they know around the classroom.

Picture Cards   Invite children to draw pictures of things around the classroom and attach word labels to each picture. Also, have them cut out pictures from magazines and catalogues and glue them onto cards. You or the child write the name of each object under each picture. Then play games with the cards.

Informing Parents About Environmental Words

Encourage parents to make their children aware of words around the home and neighborhood. See Parent Letter 27.

Word Knowledge with Sentence Strips

Reading sentence strips is another effective way to develop knowledge of individual words. Some techniques follow.

Word Pointing   Read sentence strips to focus on individual words. Read sentence strips *to* the child while you point to each word; read sentence strips together with the child as you point to the words; re-read sentences together while you fade in and out depending on the words children recall. Finally, have children point to and identify all the words they know in familiar sentence strips.

Framing Words in Dictated Sentences   Collect several old familiar dictated sentences and have children frame words they know (by placing a finger at the beginning of the word and another finger at the end of the word). Next, ask them to frame the first words in sentences . . . then last words. Finally, you frame certain words in sentence strips and have the child name the words.

Over-Copying and Under-Copying   Copying-over and under-copying sentence strips continues to help children focus on individual words.

Word Matching   Making word cards from familiar sentence strips is a great way to develop word knowledge. To do this, make a sentence strip to match an old one and cut the new sentence strip into word cards. Then have children assemble the words back into sentences again by matching them to the original sentence strip. Also, have children create sentences of their own from these word cards.

Word Sorting   Sort the cut-up sentence strips in a number of ways, according to objects, names of people and animals, action words, and color words.

Word Chains   As children begin to recognize individual words on their sentence strips, put them onto a word chain, and then keep adding known words to the chain. To increase their understanding of individual words, invite children to draw pictures on the back of the word cards.

Dictated Booklets   Help children make word booklets of things they like. Record children's ideas while they draw or cut-out illustrations for each page. Possible titles might be: My Special Toys (train set, teddy, blocks, lawn mower, bike); People I Love (Mom, Dad, Grandma, Grandpa, Kim, Sundeep, Krista).

 Informing Parents About Ways to Develop Knowledge of Words with Sentence Strips

See Parent Letter 28 to help parents develop word awareness with personal dictated sentence strips.

Developing Knowledge of Words in Predictable Literature

Reading Aloud   Many literature selections are ideal for developing knowledge of words very naturally. Find selections that have minimal print on each page such as a single word, phrase, or sentence and vivid illustrations that give many clues regarding the meaning of the text. A good example of such a book is *Does a Kangaroo Have a Mother Too?* by Eric Carle (2000), where certain words on each page are highlighted in color. Simply reading texts like this aloud to children over and over often makes them aware of individual words, especially when teachers point to each highlighted word in the text.

Literature Selections That Develop Word Knowledge

Many pattern literature selections draw specific attention to individual words by emphasizing certain words in some way.

Alphabet Books   Alphabet books usually focus on individual words effectively. The alphabet book *On Market Street* by Anita Lobel (1981) is a good example.

• *Make alphabet books:* Have the class compose their own alphabet book based on people they know or animals they are familiar with and have children illustrate each page.

Highlighted Words   In the book *Muddle Cuddle* by Laurel Dee Gugler (1997) certain words are set apart from the rest of the text in bold type (**Teddy**, **Kitty**, **Clown** . . .), which helps children identify individual words.

• Similarly, the book *There Was an Old Woman* by Stephen Wyllie and Maureen Roffey (1985) helps young readers focus on individual words because words identifying objects and characters are written on flaps that children can lift up revealing illustrations of each particular object.

• *Word cards:* As children begin to recognize individual words, write known words onto cards and have children illustrate them.

Theme Books

Books with themes also focus on particular types of words. Following are selections that draw attention to names of body parts, concept words, descriptive words, action words, colors and numbers, animals (farm, zoo, country), and insects. Additional theme books are listed in Appendix D.

Literature and Body Parts   Body parts (arms, head, thumb) are featured in books like, *This Old Man* by Pamela Adams (1974), *The Hokey Pokey* by Larry La Prise, Charles Macak, and Taftt Baker (1997);

- *Names of body parts:* Invite children to draw and label their own body parts.

Concept Books   Several books lend themselves to developing understanding of concept words such as *over, under, through, beside,* etc. Look for *Hide and Snake* by Keith Baker (1991), *Sail Away* by Donald Crews (1995), or *Where's Spot?* by Eric Hill (1994).

- *Story map:* Invite children to create their own story using prepositions (*over, under, on, in*).

Descriptive Words   Descriptive words such as *fierce, grumpy, scary, naughty* are used in *Dear Zoo* by Rod Campbell (1982) and in *Quick as a Cricket* by Audrey Wood (1982) to describe various animals (*quick, small, slow*).

- *Class chart:* Invite the class to list interesting words from familiar stories.

Action Words   Action words (*blink, sniff, snap, chew*) are used in the book *I Can Blink* by Frank Asch (1997). The story *The Wheels on the Bus* by Kovalski (1987) also emphasize actions (*swish, toot, clink*).

- *Action word list:* Have the class dictate a list of action words they find in stories read to them or in books they read themselves.

Color Words   Color words are found in a number of literature selections: *Hello Red Fox* by Eric Carle (1998) and *Let's Go Visiting* by Sue Williams (1998).

- *Color books:* Invite children to make their own color books by drawing things of different colors and dictating a label for each page.

Number Words   Numerous books develop concepts of numbers. Two of my favorites are *Two by Two* by Barbara Reid (1992) and *One More Bunny* by Rick Walton (2000).

- *Number books:* Invite partners to work together to create a number book of their own with pictures for each page.

Farm Animal Words   Farm animals are named in pattern books like *Are You My Baby?* by Cindy Chang (1996) and *Hattie and the Fox* by Mem Fox (1992).

• *Farm animal books:* have children make their own farm animal book by drawing pictures of farm animals and labeling them.

Zoo Animals   Zoo animals are named in many pattern books as well. Look for the books *I Can Roar* by Frank Asch (1985) and *Does a Kangaroo Have a Mother Too?* by Eric Carle (2000).

• *Zoo Animal Word Cards:* Have children make a number of zoo animal word cards with pictures of zoo animals on the front and labels of each animal on the back.

Animal Words   Numerous literature selections reinforce knowledge of animal names. A variety of names of animals are noted in Jonathan London's books *Wiggle Waggle* (1999) and *Snuggle Wuggle* (2000).

• Make a class list of animals.

• Have children sort animal word cards according to different categories: large, small animals; zoo, farm, woodland animals; color of animals.

• Have children make their own animal booklet by drawing an animal on each page and labeling it.

Insect Words   Eric Carle has written several pattern books with the theme of insects. Consider *The Very Lonely Firefly,* (1995) and *The Very Quiet Cricket,* (1990).

• *Insect book:* Read several books about insects to the class and then ask them to make a booklet of insects with a drawing of an insect on each page, label it and put the pages together to make booklets. See Appendix D for theme selections.

Informing Parents About Fostering Word Knowledge with Literature

Parent Letter 29 provides parents with procedures for promoting word knowledge with literature selections.

RECOGNIZING LETTERS OF THE ALPHABET

Although most children recognize some letters of the alphabet and are likely able to sing the ABC song before they enter school, teachers can reinforce this knowledge when they draw attention to letters in children's names, when they read alphabet books, read pattern literature to them, label objects, and have children copy-over and copy-under sentences. However, particular attention to individual letters can also be accomplished by playing "I Spy" games, finding letters in stories that begin with children's names, and naming letters in words children already know on their word chains. Specific strategies follow.

Letters in Names   One of the best ways to make children aware of individual letters is to start with their names.

- *Beginning Letters:* Point out the name of the letter that comes at the beginning of their name (*A* is for Amy; *N* is for Nathan, *K* is for Kody).
- *I Spy:* Play "I Spy" by having children try to find the first letters of their names on signs around the classroom, school, in titles of books, in pattern literature, and in dictated sentences and stories.

Individual Letters in Names   Focus on one letter at a time in a child's name and repeat the above activities.

Copying Letters in Names   Reinforce knowledge of letters in children's names by having children copy over the letters in their names. When their coordination develops, have them copy under the letters in their name.

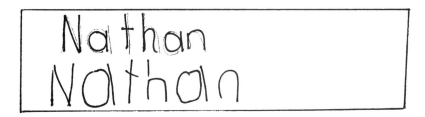

Names of Friends and Family   Once children have become aware of letters in their own name, have them become familiar with letters in the names of their friends and family. Invite children to choose the name and letter they want to work on and then repeat the activities above.

Alphabet Books

Alphabet books are great resources for helping children recognize letters of the alphabet. Try some of these activities.

Enjoyment   First, read alphabet books just for fun to develop a general awareness of letters.

Finger Tracing   During the reading of another alphabet book, focus on one letter at a time and have children name it, have them trace their fingers around letters, and name animals or objects that begin with that letter. Focus on one new letter every day or so.

Alphabet Posters   Invite children to make alphabet posters using all the letters they know. They draw or cut out pictures of things that begin with certain letters they recognize. For example, at the top of a page put a letter they know (*R*) and have them draw things or cut objects out of magazines that begin with that letter (*rake, robin, rabbit*). Once they have glued their pictures onto the paper, have them help you label each item.

Letter Hunts   Invite children to find letters they know in a variety of places such as dictated sentences, charts, pattern literature, newspapers, and magazines.

• *Pattern literature:* After you have read pattern selections a number of times, play "I Spy" by having children find words that begin with a new letter you have introduced.

• *Newspapers, magazines:* Invite children to circle particular letters they know. Another time, put seldom used letters (*z, x, q*) at the top of a page in the newspaper and have them find and circle these letters.

Word Cards   Have children sort their words from their word chain according to letters they know: find all the words that begin with the letter *N* as in *no* (*name, nickel, number, neck*); find all the words that begin with a *T* as in *telephone* (*top, tip, ten, table*) or end in the letter *P* (*map, sap, lip*).

Recognizing Letters in Dictated Stories and Sentences   Read together familiar sentence strips and then have the child point to letters they know and then you point to letters in words and have the child name the letter.

• *Spelling:* When you record new dictated sentences and stories, ask children to name letters they know to help you with the spelling of some of the words.

Informing Parents About How to Make Their Children Aware of Letters

Parents can also help their children become aware of letters by following these same strategies above. Send home Parent Letter 30 so that parents can reinforce knowledge of letters.

DEVELOPING GRAPHOPHONIC KNOWLEDGE

There are essentially two different ways to help children become aware of graphophonic principles, the ways in which sounds and letters relate to each other. One is through direct instruction and formal activities and the other is to learn letter/sound principles within the context of print that has meaning for children. In the direct instruction approach, teachers generally follow guidelines from commercial reading programs and phonics programs where children engage in numerous skill activities often separate from material they read. While there is no real harm in the direct approach, children seem to respond to phonics instruction more positively when it's connected to meaningful reading material.

Phonics: Direct Instructional Activities

Here, graphophonic instruction is introduced formally and systematically letter by letter starting with sound/symbol relationships. Children engage in numerous activities to learn the graphophonic concepts introduced and these activities are reinforced through formal drills and worksheet activities. Some of these activities follow.

I Spy   Play "I Spy" by saying, "I spy something that begins like, 'Sunday.'" Then children name things (*sun, snowman, sick*). If children choose something with the correct sound (*celery, city*) but the wrong initial letter, say "*celery* and *city* do start with the same sound as *Sunday*." It is not necessary to correct them, since the goal is to identify beginning sounds although, depending on the child's sophistication, you can certainly show them, on the spot, how sometimes *c* sounds like *s* and sometimes like a *k*.

Clap for Sounds   Ask children to clap their hands when they hear particular sounds for the beginning and ending sounds of words. Say "Listen for the ending sound in the word *hat*" (*cat, cut, hit, set*).

Circling Pictures   Children circle pictures on worksheets that begin with particular sound/symbols; circle pictures that begin with *p* (*pink, pig, picture*).

Drawing Pictures   Children draw pictures of things that begin with an *M* (*marbles, mat, milk, mom*) and draw pictures of things that end with *d* sound (*dad, rod, weed, ride*).

Naming Words   Children name things that begin like *bat* (*back, blackboard, broom, basketball*), and name words that end like *cup* (*hop, tap, step, help*).

Alphabet Cans   Set out alphabet cans by labeling empty juice cans with letter/sound symbols. Children collect objects that begin with that sound and put them into the can. Introduce a new letter every few days.

Going on a Trip   One child begins by saying, "I'm going on a trip and I'm going to pack my suitcase with things that begin like *apple*" (*animal*); the next person names something that begins like *ball* (*bun*); a third person names something that begins like *car* (*cat*). The game continues until all the letters of the alphabet are used.

Word Families   Teachers and children make lists of words that have similar rimes like: -*at* (*cat, mat, rat, fat, sat*); -*un* (*run, bun, sun, fun*).

Developing Graphophonic Knowledge Through Context

Another way to introduce sound/symbol relationships to children is by connecting the phonics activity to a context familiar to them. For example, when phonics activities relate to reading material they are familiar with (predictable literature, Big Books, dictated stories, sentence strips, or chart stories), graphophonic principles simply make more sense to children. Following are specific activities that draw children's attention to sound/symbol relationships within the context of meaningful literary experiences. While there is no prescribed sequence for introducing certain letters before others, it's often easier to begin with the letters that represent the first letters of the children's own names. Then, consider introducing easily recognizable letter/sound symbols (*M, P, T, S*); next, other initial sound symbols (*B, D, F*); and then somewhat more difficult sound/symbols (*H, L, N, R*); and finally, to less frequently used sound symbols (*V, W, X, Y, Z*). Reserve special minilessons to deal with letters that have more than one sound (*C, G, J, K*). Introduce initial sounds first, then make children aware of final consonants before addressing middle consonants. Introduce vowels (*A, E, I, O, U*) once children are familiar with consonants. Consider the following strategies for introducing children to consonants and vowels:

Children's Names   Once children recognize letters in their names, draw attention to sounds that initial letters in their names make. Then play "I Spy" by having children try to find the first letters of their names in titles of books, in pattern literature, in texts of dictated sentences and stories, and on signs around the classroom and school. Although children may be able to recognize letters, they may not be able to recognize words themselves. So have them attempt the letter sounds and you tell them what the words are if they don't know them.

Names of Family and Friends   Once children have become aware of initial sounds in their own names, have them become familiar with sounds of letters in names of their family, pets, and friends. Invite them to choose a friend's name and find words with those beginning letters in stories, on charts, and signs around the classroom.

Alphabet Books   At first, read alphabet books for enjoyment. But then have children pay particular attention to certain letters that have easily distinguishable sounds such as *M, P, T,* and *S.* Invite children to name all the items that begin with these letter/sounds in the alphabet book. When reading other alphabet books, introduce a new initial letter/sound each day. Again, read names of items in the books beginning with those particular letter/sounds, emphasizing particular initial sounds.

Pattern Literature   After reading familiar pattern selections a number of times, play "I Spy" by having children find words that begin with the same sound as the letter you name (*B, D, F*).

Word Cards   Have children sort their cards of known words according to initial sound/symbols they know. Find all the words that begin with the letter *R* as in *roll* (*rake, rabbit, run*); find all the words that begin with *N* as in *not* (*new, numbers, no, nine*). Find words that begin with the letter *M* as in *mat, D* as in *donut, G* as in *Grandma* and *Grandpa,* etc.

Dictating Stories and Sentences   Have children point to letter/sounds they know in familiar sentence strips and have them name the letter and the sound it makes.

• Spelling: When recording new dictated sentences and stories, ask children to name letters they know to help with the spelling of words.

Alphabet Posters   Invite children to make alphabet posters using letters and sound/symbols they know (*M, P, T, S*). They can draw or cut out pictures of things that begin with certain letter/sounds they recognize. For example, at the top of a page make the initial letter *P.* Then children draw or find pictures of things beginning with that letter. Once they have glued their pictures on, help them label each item.

I Spy   Play "I Spy" around the classroom for words and items they see. You start by saying, "I spy something that begins like the word *telephone.*" Then list all these things on a chart (*table, tack, tape, toys*).

Poetry   Read poetry selections with rhyme to the class and have them guess the rhyming words at the end of each line. Children love doing this with poems in the book of poems *Alligator Pie* by Dennis Lee (1987).

Word Families   Choose words found in familiar literature, poetry, and songs and create word families. For example, in the story "Cat on the Mat" by Brian Wildsmith (1982), make word families for the word *cat* (*bat, cat, hat, sat*).

• *Create New Rhymes:* Have children dictate or write new versions of poems. Children in Wayne Gingrich's class wrote the following poem based on "Alligator Pie" by Dennis Lee (1987).

> Apple Sauce
>
> Apple sauce, apple sauce.
> If I don't get some
> it's going to make me cross.
> Give away some candy,
> Give away my floss,
> But don't give away my
>   apple sauce.

Continue the same procedure with other poems from *Alligator Pie*. Similarly, make new rhymes with trade books that are written in rhyme like *Good Night* by Jan Pienkowski (1999) or *Bugs for Lunch* by Margery Facklam (1999).

Informing Parents About Phonic Principles in Context

Most parents are concerned about making their children aware of phonic principles, so send Parent Letter 31 home so they can reinforce these concepts at home.

GUIDED READING: STRATEGIES LEADING TO INDEPENDENCE

Guided reading strategies lead young children safely and securely toward independent reading. Guided reading gives support to young readers because children work in small groups to read together materials already familiar to them with the teacher as a guide to give help when needed. The support from peers and the teacher builds confidence allowing children to take safe risks in their journey toward independence. At the same time, guided reading allows children the freedom to read without assistance. In the guided reading process, children read material that is already familiar to them such as predictable pattern literature, Big Books, poetry, and refrain books that were already read to them during read-aloud sessions and shared reading. Unfamiliar material is introduced gradually once children read old familiar material with confidence. Guided reading provides the scaffold required to move into the independent phase. The guided reading activities are planned for youngsters who have begun to read some material independently such as personal sentence strips, chart stories, and predictable pattern literature and recognize fifty or more individual words.

Like read-aloud strategies, the guided reading process involves building comprehension, using reading strategies (meaning, word patterns, and phonics), word study, phonics study, and interpretive activities. But unlike read-aloud sessions where teachers read the selections to the children, in guided reading children are expected to read themselves, in unison, with partners, and individually. The following guided reading procedures are intended to be used first with familiar easy-to-read materials (predictable pattern selections and easy-read refrain books) before moving to more difficult text found in traditional refrain books and complex picture books. Children should continue to read familiar predictable text until they read it with ease before moving to unfamiliar text. Similarly, once they are able to read *familiar* refrain books and complex picture books, they move on to unfamiliar ones.

I offer a note of caution regarding the amount of instructional time spent in the guided reading process. Guided reading strategies are intended to be used sparingly, perhaps every third day so that on alternative days there is lots of time for children to independently explore, select, and read books on their own. The ultimate goal is to move toward individualized, independent reading as soon as possible so that eventually guided reading will no longer be necessary.

GUIDED READING WITH PREDICTABLE LITERATURE FOR SMALL GROUPS

Invite five or six children who are able to read some text independently and conduct a guided reading session with them.

Setting the Stage

Choose numerous predictable pattern selections that have already been used for reading aloud, shared reading, Big Books, and chart stories. Start with predictable selections with minimal print first (*I Can Blink Like an Owl*, Frank Asch, 1997; *Wiggle Waggle*, Jonathan London, 1999; *Let's Go Visiting*, Sue Williams, 1998).

Reading the Cover   Invite children to read in unison the title, name of the author and illustrator, and talk about other books by this author and illustrator.

Reading the Selection   Invite the children to read the selection in unison. Next, have the group re-read the text in different ways:

• Two-part reading: Half the group reads the narration and the other half reads the refrain;

• Partner reading: Partners read selections together;

• Role reading: Individual children read narrations and another child reads the refrain;

• Individual reading: Individual children read whole selections independently;

• Cueing Systems: When children have difficulty with words, encourage them to use meaning (semantic) strategies (look at the pictures, recall the story, think what would make sense). If they have difficulty with words in the repeated lines (syntax) ask them to think about the pattern in the story. Have them use the phonic strategy for words that have easily identifiable initial sounds (*M, P, S, T, B, D, F, H, L, N, R*). Ask, "What sound does this letter make?"

Word Study   Study words in the selection by the following:

- Frame all the names of characters in the story;
- Find all the action words;
- Find descriptive words, color words;
- Find words in the story that begin with certain sounds/symbols;
- Find words in the story that end with certain sounds/symbols.

Comprehension   Talk about the book and have the children examine the predictable features of the selection (repeated lines, beautiful illustrations, rhythm, rhyme) and have the children discuss other books that have these features.

Follow-up Activities   Have children practice reading the book of the day and then go to the reading corner to read books on their own such as familiar predictable pattern selections, group charts, and Big Books.

Informing Parents About How to Guide Early Readers

Parent Letter 32 provides parents with information about how to guide their children in guided reading.

GUIDED READING WITH UNFAMILIAR PREDICTABLE PATTERN LITERATURE

Reading unfamiliar predictable pattern literature is reserved for children who read numerous familiar pattern selections and dictated stories fluently. Many teachers code literature selections in some way so that children are able to locate predictable pattern texts easily.

Setting the Stage

Choose selections that have enlarged print so children can see the text easily or have several copies of single selections available so that each child has a copy to read. Again use selections that have many features of predictability (minimal print on each page, bright illustrations, repeated patterns, rhyme, and rhythm). Try selections like *Snuggle Wuggle* (Jonathan

London, 2000); *On Market Street* (Arnold Lobel, 1981); *From Head to Toe* (Eric Carle, 1997); *I Went Walking* (Sue Williams, 1990).

Study the Cover   Have the children read the cover including the title, names of the author, and illustrator. Talk about the other books written by this author or illustrated by this illustrator.

Focus Question   Since this is a new book, ask the children to think about something while they read the story. Choose *one* of these focus questions: think about problems in the story; think about characters and how they are different; think about whether the events in the story seem realistic; think about the structure of the story.

Reading the Text   Since this selection is new to the children, you read it the first time. Then have the children read the piece in different ways:

• Children read the selection together in unison;

• Half the group reads the narration while the other half reads the refrain;

• Partners read the whole selection;

• Volunteers read the selection;

• Children read the selection to reading buddies, parent volunteers, and peers.

• Help children employ various cueing systems for words they don't know, by asking them to think about what would make sense (semantics/ meaning); what pattern they notice (syntax/patterns of language); and the sound the initial letter in the troublesome word makes (phonics/ sound/symbol relationships).

Word Study   Study some of the words in the selection as a group:

• Frame all the names of the characters in the story;

• Find all the action words in the story;

• Find all the descriptive words in the story;

• Find words in the story that begin with certain sound/symbols;

• Find words that end with common sound/symbols.

Comprehension   First have a discussion about the focus question (the events in the story and if they seemed real). Then give the children the option of going to the reading corner to practice reading the book of the day or other predictable pattern selections. Alternatively, invite the children to interpret the story through art activities:

- With paper plates, create a puppet of one of the characters in the story;

- Make a portrait of one of the characters in the story using construction paper, tissue paper, paint, crayon, markers, pastels;

- Model a character in the story with plasticine or play dough.

- Alternative art activities: Refer to the section *Learning Activities for Centers* in Chapter Two.

GUIDED READING WITH FAMILIAR AND UNFAMILIAR EASY-READ REFRAIN BOOKS (LOW DENSITY PRINT)

Once children are able to read both familiar and unfamiliar predictable pattern selections successfully, encourage them to read easy-read refrain books. Start with selections that are familiar to children such as those read during the read-aloud sessions. First read easy-read refrain books with lots of illustrations and a moderate amount of print before reading traditional refrain books with dense print.

Setting the Stage

For group reading, use familiar selections. Look for selections that have large print so that everyone in the group can see the text. Alternatively, have a text set of the same selection so children can follow along. Occasionally easy-read refrain selections from commercial reading programs are appropriate, providing they are unabridged and retain the rich language of the original piece.

Easy-Read Refrain Books   Start with easy-read refrain books with moderately dense print and lots of illustrations because they are easier for young children to read. Several selections come to mind: *Hattie and the Fox* (Mem Fox, 1992); *Mortimer* (Robert Munsch, 1985). Several books by Eric Carle also have refrains such as *The Very Busy Spider* (1984); *The Very Quiet Cricket* (1990); *The Very Hungry Caterpillar* (1997); *The Very Lonely Firefly* (1997). See Appendix D for other easy-read refrain books.

Examining Covers   Have the children read the cover including the title, and name of the author and illustrator. Have a discussion about other books they know that have refrains in them.

Focus Question   Ask the children to think about *one* question as they read the selection: think about one of the characters and all the things you learn about them; think about the problems in the story; think about the events and whether they seem real; what did the author need to know to write this book?; think about other literature selections this story reminds you of.

Reading the Text   Invite the group to read the selection in different ways:

• Teachers and children read the selection together;

• The children read the selection together in unison;

• Half the group reads the narrative and the other half reads the refrain;

• One child reads the narration and the group reads the refrain;

• Individual children volunteer to read the story alone.

• Cueing Systems: Help children use various cueing systems for words they are unsure of by thinking about meaning (semantic) strategies first (what would make sense here; look at the pictures to give you clues). Encourage children to use word order (syntax) strategies to figure out whether an object or an action is required for the sentence to make sense. Ask children about the beginning sounds of words (phonics) to give them clues.

Word Study   Study some of the words in the selection as a group and try one or two of the following:

• Frame names of characters, action words, description words in the story;

• Frame words that begin or end with certain sounds/symbols; check the story for words found in it that have same initial sound. For example, in the story *Mortimer* have the children frame words that begin with *M*, *S*, and *D*.

• Create word families from words in the story *Mortimer*, for example *bed, red, led, fed*.

Comprehension Discussion   Talk about the Focus Question (think about problems in the story). Then have a general discussion.

• *General discussion:* Also discuss *one* of these questions: what are the characteristics of a character you liked? In what ways does this story remind you of something that has happened to you?

Follow-Up Activities   Have children practice reading the easy-read refrain book of the day alone or with a friend; read other easy-read refrain books in the reading corner.

• Encourage children to choose a writing activity after reading a story in the reading corner. Post these activities in the reading corner.

• Dictate or write your own refrain book;

• Write a menu for a character in one of the refrain books;

• Write a postcard to the author telling them what you think of the book;

• Write a bumper sticker to advertise a favorite book.

Unfamiliar Easy-Read Refrain Books

Repeat this same procedure for easy-read refrain books that are unfamiliar to the children.

GUIDED READING WITH FAMILIAR AND UNFAMILIAR TRADITIONAL REFRAIN BOOKS

Once children are able to read both familiar and unfamiliar easy-read refrain books with confidence, encourage them to read traditional refrain books with higher density print. Start with selections that are familiar to the children that have been read to them during the read-aloud sessions. Many traditional refrain books include *The Little Red Hen*, *The Three Little Pigs*, *The Three Billy Goats Gruff*, and *The Three Bears*.

Setting the Stage

For group reading, use familiar selections the children have heard before during read-aloud sessions. Have several copies of the same selection so children can follow along in their own book. Also look for refrain selections in commercial reading programs, only if they are unabridged, and written by a recognizable author.

Examining Covers   Have the children read the cover including the title, and name of the author and illustrator. Have a discussion about what they know about the structure of traditional refrain books. Start a chart listing these features (characters often come in sets of three; characters are either really good or really bad; there are usually three key events).

Focus Question   Ask the children to think about the characteristics of traditional refrain books as they read the story.

Reading the Text   Invite the group to read the selection in different ways:

- Teachers and children read the selection together;

- The children read the selection together in unison;

- One child reads the narration and the group reads the refrain;

- Individual children take on the role of characters in the story and the whole group reads the refrain;

- Individual children volunteer to read parts of the story alone.

- Help children use various cueing systems for words they have trouble with by having them think about the meaning (semantic strategy). Ask, "What word would make sense here?" "Go back and read the sentence again and think about what would make sense." "Look at the pictures to give you clues." Encourage children to use word order (syntax) strategies to figure out whether an object or an action word is required for the sentence to make sense. Ask children about the beginning sounds of words (phonics) to give them clues to unknown words or use rimes in words they know to figure out unknown words. For example *uck* in *duck* will help to figure out the word *muck*.

Word Study   Study some of the words in the selection as a group and try one or two of these activities:

- Frame names of characters, action words, description words in the story;

- Talk about what certain phrases in traditional tales mean. "What does it mean when mother pig sent her pigs to 'seek their fortunes'?"; "What do you think the word *fetched* means?"; "In the story *The Three Bears*, what are the words to describe things that are really big (*huge, great, large*)?"; "What are words that describe small things (*wee, tiny, little*)?"

- Frame words that begin or end with certain sound/symbols (*B, D, F*);

- Create word families from words in the story *The Three Billy Goats Gruff* (*him, bin, din, fin*).

Comprehension Discussion   Talk about the focus question (the characteristics of refrain books) and have the children add information to the chart of features of traditional refrain books. Each time you read a traditional refrain book, add new information to the chart.

• *General discussion:* Also discuss *one* of these questions: describe a character you liked, or didn't like. In what ways do the problems in the story seem real?

Follow-up Activities   Have children choose an activity in which to engage:

• Practice reading the traditional refrain book of the day alone or with a friend; read other traditional refrain books in the reading corner. They may also like to interpret stories through drama activities such as:

• *Charades:* Pretend to be a character in one of the traditional refrain books and have the children in the group guess who you are;

• Use props from the drama box and act out one of the refrain stories;

• *Role play:* Pretend you are baby bear and find your favorite chair broken;

• *Telephone conversation:* Pretend you are the wolf in *The Three Little Pigs* and call the little pig and try to convince her that you are really a nice guy.

Unfamiliar Traditional Refrain Books

Repeat this same procedure for unfamiliar traditional refrain books with high density print.

• Alternative Literature Response Activities: Refer to the section *Learning Activities for Centers* outlined in Chapter Two and *Ways to Respond to Literature* in Chapter Three.

GUIDED READING WITH COMPLEX PICTURE BOOKS

Once children are able to read numerous predictable pattern selections and refrain books successfully, encourage them to read complex picture books. Start with selections that are familiar to children that have been read to them during previous read-aloud sessions.

Setting the Stage

Have several copies of single selections available so that each child has their own copy to read. Selections from commercial reading programs may be used as long as the stories are not abridged and remain true to the original versions.

Examining Covers   Have a discussion about the cover and talk about other books they know by this author or illustrator.

Focus Question   Since the children have already heard the story before, have them think about *one* major aspect of the story while they read: think about problems characters had in the story; think about characters and how they are different; think about events in the story and whether they seemed logical; what did this story make you think about?; what features of this story do you particularly enjoy?

Reading the Selection   Read the story in a number of ways:

• You and the children read the selection together in unison. Fade out when the children are able to read on their own.

• The children read the selection together in unison;

• *Reading parts:* The children take on the role of certain characters and read aloud;

• Help children employ various cueing systems for words they have difficulty with. Help them use meaning (semantics) by asking what would make sense. Assist them with word order (syntax), by asking what kind of word would work (an object or an action word). Also encourage children to use their graphophonic skills and knowledge to "sound out" unknown words.

Word Study   Study some of the words in the selection as a group. Consider some of the following activities:

• Frame words that describe the characters;

• Frame descriptive words you like;

• Frame words in the story that begin with *H, L, N, R*;

• Frame words that end with particular sounds/symbols;

• Make a family of words (*run, bun, fun, sun*).

Comprehension   First, discuss the focus question before having a general discussion.

• Children discuss the focus question together (what were the problems characters had in this story?).

- General comprehension discussion: The children discuss *one* of the following exercises:

- Choose a character and talk about what they were like;

- Compare two different characters to see how they are similar and different;

- How are the problems in this story like the problems in other stories you have read?

Follow-up Activities   Have the children choose one of the following activities:

- At the reading corner, children read books independently;

- Invite children to respond to picture books by dictating or writing responses to them (what you enjoyed about the story; what you learned from this story, things you would change if you were the author of this story).

- Alternative Literature Response Activities: Refer to the section *Learning Activities for Centers* in Chapter Two and *Ways to Respond to Literature* found in Chapter Three.

Unfamiliar Complex Picture Books

Once children have experienced guided reading sessions with familiar picture books, follow the same process above with unfamiliar complex picture book selections.

INDIVIDUALIZED READING ACTIVITIES

One of the most interesting phenomenon about young children is the range of abilities in any one group of children. On one extreme, some youngsters have problems speaking coherently while others come to school already reading! Although all children benefit from the many activities discussed earlier, as children begin to read independently, they require additional attention. Initially these children need to be nurtured gently in order to build confidence in their newfound ability. As children become more independent, there are certain things teachers should remember. First, children continue to need to have stories read to them. Secondly, independent readers often try to read selections perfectly, so let them know that even grown-ups misread words in selections sometimes. Explain that when a word doesn't make sense, they should go back and try the sentence again. A third issue is the over-use of sounding out, which makes their reading slow and plodding. When children insist on sounding out every word, they are likely relying too heavily on phonic principles. Encourage them to think of words that would retain the meaning of the passage.

Planning for Independent Reading

As you plan for independent readers, be mindful of the following issues:

Time   Children need lots of class time to explore, look at, and read books even while they are in the Emergent and Beginning phases of reading. This time should be extended to thirty minutes each day once children begin to read selections independently.

Types of Reading Material   As children begin to read independently, it is important to make appropriate reading material available.

• Predictable pattern literature: Encourage children to read predictable pattern selections that are already familiar to them. As well, invite children to read familiar Big Books especially those they have had a hand in illustrating. Save old chart stories the class has composed and invite children to read them again. Also have available numerous selections of predictable pattern literature that is unfamiliar to the children. Organize bins of both familiar and unfamiliar predictable pattern literature according to difficulty.

• Refrain books: Build collections of two kinds of refrain books: easy-read refrain books that are supported with numerous illustrations and few words per page, and another group of traditional refrain books that have few illustrations and more dense print per page.

• Complex picture books: Have lots of complex picture books on hand for children to read. Organize picture books according to difficulty so children can access books they are able to read.

Organizing Literature   Organize the classroom reading materials according to predictable pattern literature, refrain books, and complex picture books. Code them in some way so that children can easily find selections at their reading level.

Helping Children Select Books   Before encouraging children to look at or read books in the reading corner, they may require minilessons on how to select books. Here are some ideas.

• Find books that are familiar to you that you may have heard the teacher read during read-aloud sessions or that were made into Big Books;

- Ask friends for selections they liked;

- Find books by authors you like;

- Choose books based on topics you are interested in;

- Check for interesting pictures in books to give you an idea if you might like looking at the book;

- Find books that are easy to read. If there are too many words you are unsure of, put it back and find an easier one;

- Put a book back if it is not interesting to you and find another one that is.

Procedures for the Reading Corner

- Choose a book: Have lots of books available at all levels so that children will be successful choosing books in the reading corner either to look at or read.

- Encourage children to read selections in many different ways: to themselves, teachers, parent volunteers, and reading buddies. Adults can help keep track of books read.

- It's wise to ensure that children are able to read books fluently before they take them home to practice reading them with their parents.

- Have each child record the stories they have read into a reading log.

Reading Log
Books I've Read

Josh

Date	Name of Book
Ma 2	Dear zoo
Mar 7	Brown Bear
Mar 10	I CAN BLINK

Activities for Responding to Books   Children learn so much from simply looking at and reading books so provide lots of time just to read and enjoy books. Occasionally, introduce the children to different ways to interpret the books they read. A response to a single book while at the reading center is appropriate. Post the following chart to give children ideas of ways they can respond to books:

• Look at a book and tell a story based on the pictures.

• Dictate a story by using illustrations in the book as a guide.

• Tell a friend about the book.

• Invite children to give a book talk to a small group telling the things they enjoyed about the book and things they disliked.

• Have a book talk with a friend and tell them about the book you read and invite them to you tell them about a book they liked.

• Retell the story to a friend, volunteer, or reading buddy.

• With a friend, read a group chart related to a theme or author.

• Read a familiar Big Book with a friend.

• Invite children to practice their reading of stories teachers have copied onto overhead acetates.

• Read a poem with a friend; use lots of expression.

• Read a story you have dictated to a volunteer.

• Draw various events that happened in the story in a story map.

• Make a picture book of the characters and some events in the story.

• Work with a volunteer and discuss *one* of these questions:

  1. Talk about a character you liked.
  2. Compare two different characters to see how they are similar and different;
  3. In what ways does this story remind you of something that has happened to you?
  4. How are the problems in this story like the problems in other stories you have read?

• Respond to a book you have read by dictating or writing responses to it: what you enjoyed about the story; what you learned from this story; things you would change if you were the author of this story. This activity is reserved for children who are reading independently.

• Alternative Response Ideas: Find more response ideas in the section *Learning Activities for Centers* in Chapter Two and in the section *Ways to Respond to Literature* outlined in Chapter Three.

This chapter discussed ways to support Developing and Independent readers. In the following chapter we outline ways teachers can organize informational topics, theme studies, and author studies.

Gathering the Books:
Information Books, Theme
Studies, Author Studies

ACTIVITIES FOR INFORMATIONAL BOOKS

Most young children love books that are brimming with information about topics that interest them. Information is found in nonfiction books as well as in fictional literature. In the reading corner, attractively display lots of informational books on various topics and of varying levels of difficulty to entice the children.

Value of Informational Books

Children are often more attracted to books with information because they satisfy their natural interest in certain topics. Informational books are a strong motivator for learning to read. As children look at and read informational books about particular topics that interest them, they become familiar with the vocabulary associated with the topic. I am reminded of Roye, a first grader I worked with a few years ago, who was fascinated with sharks, whales, and porpoises. For months books about these topics were the only books he signed out from the library. I was amazed that he could recognize numerous types of sharks by both their appearance and names because these books had been read to him so frequently by his mother.

Activities for Informational Books

Several activities promote reading through the use of informational materials.

Read Aloud

Select informational books to read to the class that interest most of the children or that relate to a social studies or science theme such as bears. Read one of the following selections: *Bears, Bears and More Bears* (Jackie Morris, 1995); *Time to Sleep* (Denise Fleming, 1997); or *Every Autumn Comes the Bear* (Jim Arnosky, 1993).

Cover Study   First examine the cover (*Bears, Bears, and More Bears* by Jackie Morris) and have children read the title and the name of the author and illustrator. Next, have the children study the illustration on the cover and ask them what they know about the topic from the cover illustration. Start a chart called, "What We Know About Bears." Then write down the children's ideas onto the chart: Bears eat garbage; Bears hibernate; Bears scratch trees; Bears eat fish; Bears like honey.

What We Know About the Topic   Ask the children what else they know about bears and add this information to the chart, "What We Know About Bears."

What We Want to Know About the Topic   Next, ask the children what they would like to know about the topic, bears. Write this information onto another chart called, "What We Want to Know About Bears." The children's questions may include: Why do bears fight? Why do bears hibernate? Why do bears come in different colors?

Reading for Information   As you read the selection *Bears, Bears, and More Bears* to the children, have them listen for answers to their questions and to also listen for additional information about bears.

Sharing Information Learned   After the reading, have children share information they learned as they listened to the selection and add this information to the chart. (Bears are all different sizes and colors; Bears sleep in the winter; They can climb trees and run fast).

Answers to Questions   Ask the children if they found any answers to their questions about bears and record this information on the chart, "What We Want to Know About Bears."

Additional Activities with Informational Books

Reading Informational Books About Bears   Read many more books about the topic and continue to add information to the various charts.

Information About Bears in Fiction   Find other fictional literature selections that provide information about the topic. In the case of the bear topic, read stories such as *Blueberries for Sal* (McCloskey, 1976); *Where's Bear* (Pomerantz, 1984); *Winter Bear* (Craft, 1975). After reading these stories aloud to the children have them add new information to the various charts.

Individual Dictation   Have children dictate a report outlining what they have learned about bears.

Dictated Sentence Captions   Invite children to dictate sentences to depict facts they know about bears (Bears live in forests; Bears eat berries and honey).

Charting Information   After reading several information books about bears, have the children develop informational charts to organize what they have learned about bears. Do this as a whole class activity. Invite children to dictate information and illustrate ideas for the charts.

Comparing   Invite individual children to compare two different aspects of the topic. (For instance, compare two different bears.)

Center Activities   Plan various activities related to the study of bears for the following centers: listening, speaking/drama, reading corner, writing, dictated stories, word study, and art. For ideas, refer to *Activities for Learning Centers* in Chapter Two.

Informational Selections   Information books that young children enjoy are listed in Appendix D.

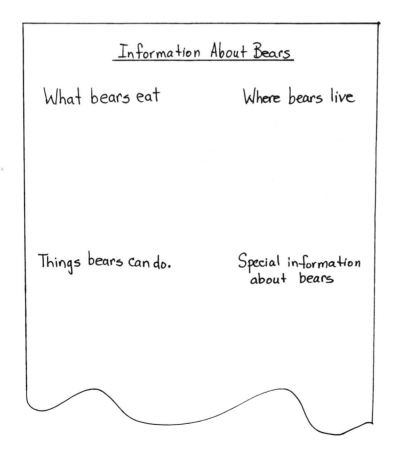

THEME STUDIES FOR YOUNG CHILDREN

Since children enjoy listening to stories about topics that interest them, develop activities to accompany various child-directed themes. Themes could be developed on a variety of topics such as the family, animals (farm, woodland), parts of the body, the neighborhood, the school, colors, language patterns, and numbers. Theme studies might also be developed around issues young children think about such as: running away from home, going to bed, family issues, friendship, etc.

Variety of Selections

Try to collect several books (10 to 20) related to a single theme. Seek out different types of selections that include predictable patterns, informational resource books, poetry, refrain books, and complex picture books. If possible, locate audiotapes and video stories on the theme.

Sources for Theme Studies

Many school districts develop their own theme units including activities and selections, so check these out before developing your own units. Also consult with your librarian and community library for resources.

Organizing Theme Activities

Over the course of approximately two weeks, plan activities such as reading aloud, shared reading sessions, reading books, and interpreting literature children read and hear.

Whole Class Activity   One way to organize these activities is to start each day with a whole class activity such as reading aloud, developing a chart story, or conducting a shared reading session.

Language Activities   After the whole class activity, children participate in learning activities to develop their language skills in listening, speaking, reading, writing, and interpreting abilities. These activities may involve: listening to audiotaped stories; reading literature in the reading corner; interpreting literature through drama and art; composing stories; word study; social studies and science exploration (refer to *Activities for Learning Centers* in Chapter Two).

Organizing Learning Activities   Learning activities are accomplished in two ways:

- Class activities: Each child participates in the same activity (everyone draws an animal and its home); the next day every child in the class looks at or reads selections related to the theme for twenty to thirty minutes; another day everyone writes a story related to the theme.

- Learning centers: Another way to organize activities is to have groups of children participate in different activities simultaneously. For example, one group composes stories; another group models woodland animals from plasticine; while another group dramatizes a scene from a story. Additional center activities are described in *Learning Activities for Centers* in Chapter Two.

Two-Week Theme Plan

Thematic units for young children generally last about ten school days. Of course, this may vary depending on the interest of the children and the number of available resources. The following generic suggestions can be used for any thematic unit with slight modifications. Theme activities are of two types: whole class activity and learning activities. Accordingly, during any one day, children will engage in a whole class activity as well as learning activities to reinforce language abilities.

Daily Theme Activities   Specific examples of these activities are outlined below.

Whole Class Activities   Start each day's session with *one* of the following whole class activities: reading aloud, whole class chart story, or the shared reading process. Over the course of two weeks all three strategies are used.

- Read-Aloud Session: On one day read aloud one selection related to the theme. Follow the read-aloud process outlined earlier in this book.

- Whole Class Chart Story: Another way to begin the language arts session is to develop chart stories related to concepts in the theme. During an animal theme, for example, develop a chart regarding a cow and list what it looks like (ears, nose, eyes, body); what it eats; where it lives; how it helps us. Other topics for chart stories might be: comparing two specific animals such as ducks and chicks and listing how they are the same and how they are different; another chart story could compare farm animals to pets regarding where they live, what they eat, what they can do, problems they may have.

- Shared Reading: Another option for the whole class activity is the shared reading process outlined earlier.

Learning Activities for Theme Studies

Center activities are very effective in thematic studies where small groups of children engage in different activities. The following activities are planned with learning centers in mind. Only a few examples are provided here, since a more complete list of center activities is found in the section *Learning Activities for Centers* in Chapter Two.

Listening Center Activities   At the listening center, place audiotapes of stories related to the theme for children to listen to. Invite children to participate in only *one* activity.

- Listen for problems in the story and discuss them in your group;

- With a partner, talk about two different characters and compare them.

Speaking/Drama Center Activities   In the drama/speaking center, invite children to participate in *one* of the following activities:

- Play charades by making actions of a character and having the rest of the group guess what it is;

- Mime a situation in a story and have the group guess the story.

Art Center   At the art center have children engage in *one* of the following activities:

- Make a puppet of a favorite character in a book from construction materials (paper bags, paper plates, boxes).

- With plasticine, play dough, or clay invite children to model a character from a story.

Word Study Center   At the word study center, place chart stories, theme word cards, magazines, newspapers, and sentence strips. Have children do *one* of the following activities:

- Cut out pictures to match the theme words on word cards (farm animals: horse, pig, duck);

- On a magazine page, circle all the words that begin with the letter at the beginning of a theme word *duck* (*dog, dish, door*); circle words that end with the sound at the end of the theme word *cat* (*rabbit, cart, pet*).

Dictation Center   At the dictation center, invite a parent volunteer to record children's compositions related to the following activities:

- Dictate what you remember of a story related to the theme and read it with a parent volunteer or reading buddy;

- Dictate a new story about the theme topic.

Writing/ Composing Center   At the writing center invite the children to do *one* of the following composing activities:

- Cut out objects related to the theme study (*pets: dogs, cats, goldfish*) and label them;

- Write your own story related to the theme using all the skills you know in spelling. Try to spell as best you can and don't bother other people to help with spelling words.

Reading Corner   In the reading corner fill the area with all kinds of books including predictable pattern books, refrain books, poetry, songs, Big Books, charts, information books, and complex picture books. Place all the theme-related books in a special bin so children can find them easily. Ask a parent volunteer to work in this center to read to children or listen while children read to them. Also, have other students record the selections they have read in a personal log.

Invite children to do *one* of the following:

- Dictate a story by using illustrations as a guide;

- Read a group chart with a friend related to the theme;

- Read a poem about the theme with a friend; use lots of expression.

Literature Selections for Early Years Themes

Several theme selections are listed in Appendix D for themes such as farm animals, family, friendship, parts of the body, language concepts, colors, and mathematics.

AUTHOR STUDIES FOR YOUNG CHILDREN

Young children very quickly become attached to particular authors and want to hear their stories over and over. Books by Eric Carle are favorites for kindergartners and early readers because of their repeated features, refrains, and colorful illustrations. Donald Crews' books are also popular with young children because each illustration tells a complete story by itself while the text of one or two words per page simply reinforces the pictures. Another author the youngest learners enjoy is Margaret Wise Brown, because the concepts in her stories are universal. Also see Appendix D for additional selections.

Variety of Selections

Try to collect several books related to a single author. Seek out different types of selections that include predictable patterns, as well as complex picture books. Also, locate audiotapes and video stories of a particular author's work.

Sources for Author Studies

Many school districts develop their own author kits including activities and selections, so check these out before developing your own. Also, consult with your school and community librarians for resources. Many authors also have websites and the older students enjoy visiting them.

Kinds of Selections

Children in the early years will likely enjoy material that they can read for themselves, so choose authors who write material that is very predictable (repeated lines, refrains, strong rhythm and rhyme).

Organizing Author Studies

Over the course of a week or two, plan whole class activities such as reading aloud, chart stories, and shared reading sessions. After the whole class activity, have children participate in comprehension activities to interpret one of the author's selections.

Read-Aloud Session   Start with reading aloud several selections of a particular author. Follow the read-aloud process outlined earlier in this book, which involves:

• Having children read the title, name of the author, and illustrator from the book.

• Posing a broad question to focus children's listening. In an author study, draw attention to the characteristics of the author's style.

• Reading the selection aloud to the class.

• Having the children discuss the characteristics of the author's books. List their ideas onto a chart (characters are usually animals, pictures are really bright, there are repeated lines, there's rhyme). Each time a new story is read by the same author add new information to the chart.

• Inviting children to participate in comprehension activities that are organized in two different ways: each child in the class participates in the same activity; or the activities are organized in learning centers where small groups of children participate in different activities simultaneously. For example, one group composes a story using the features of the author; another group illustrates one of the characters in one of the books by the author using the same art medium as the illustrator did; at the listening center another group listens to an audiotape of selections by the author.

Shared Reading Session   At the beginning of another day, consider having a shared reading session as the whole class activity. It involves:

• Reading aloud predictable pattern literature;

• Reading the piece in unison;

• Making a Big Book;

• Examining words, letters, and sound/symbol relationships;

• Interpreting stories in a variety of ways.

Learning Activities for Author Studies

Following are activities that can be adapted to a variety of author studies. The following are planned with learning centers in mind. Only a few activities are listed here since a comprehensive list of activities are included in the section *Learning Activities for Centers* in Chapter Two.

Listening Center Activities   At the listening center place several audiotapes of stories written by the author for children to listen to. Invite them to complete *one* of the following:

• Listen for problems in the story. How is the problem in this story similar or different from problems in other books by this author? Discuss in your group.

• With a partner, compare two books by the same author. How are they the same or different?

Drama/Speaking Center   In the drama/speaking center have the children use various props (old hats, scarves, large cloths for capes, tents, shawls) to interpret stories by the author. Invite them to participate in *one* of the following activities:

• Mime a situation in a story by this author and have the group guess the story;

• With a partner, role play a telephone conversation between you and the author and tell the author what you liked or didn't like about their stories.

Art Center   At the art center, place a variety of different media and invite children to be involved in *one* of the following activities:

• Collage making: With construction paper, cut or tear paper to create a character or scene from a book by this author;

• Invite children to make a character from a story by this author with plasticine, play dough, or clay.

Word Study Center   At the word study center, place chart stories, magazines, newspapers, markers, scissors, glue, blank paper, and sentence strips. Have children do *one* of the following activities:

• Cut out pictures to match words on word cards from stories by this author;

• Sort word cards according to kind of animals, color, action, objects;

• On a magazine page, circle all the words that begin with the sound at the beginning of *man*; circle words that end with the sound in the word *calf*.

Dictation Center   At the dictation center, have children dictate sentences and stories related to the following activities. Have them select *one* activity.

• Invite the children to dictate a letter to the author telling what you like about their books.

• Have the children dictate bumper stickers advertizing this author's books.

Writing/Composing Center   At the writing center, have children engage in *one* of the following activities.

• Make a birthday card for this author or one of the characters in their books.

- Write your own story based on the structure of a story by this author using all the skills you know in spelling. Try to spell as best you can on your own.

Reading Corner   In the reading corner, set up a display of selections by this author along with all kinds of books by other authors including predictable pattern books, refrain books, poetry, songs, Big Books, charts, information books, and complex picture books. While the children are in the reading corner they read *one* book by the author as well as books from several other authors. Ask a parent volunteer to work in this center to read to children or listen while they read to them. Also, have children record the selections they have read in a personal log.

Invite children to do *one* of the following:

- Look at a book by this author.

- Read a group chart related to this author with a friend.

- Read a Big Book by this author with a friend.

Authors and Selections

Several authors are perennial favorites with young children. They include: Paulette Bourgeois, Eric Carle, Donald Crews, Mirra Ginsberg, Eric Hill, Arnold Lobel, Mercer Mayer, Robert Munsch, Margaret Wise Brown, and Charlotte Zolotow. A complete list of their books is found in Appendix D.

This chapter provided teachers with ideas for organizing informational units, theme studies, and author studies. Chapter Six outlines ways to assess children's progress in literacy and makes suggestions for communicating effectively with parents.

6

Assessing Student Progress and Communicating with Parents

ASSESSING STUDENT PROGRESS

Assessing student progress in the early years is a complex process that takes into account many factors: economic conditions of families; the diversity of families; differences among the abilities and interests of young learners; developmental aspects of learning; attitudes toward assessment; a focus on positive versus negative growth of individual children; understanding progress over long periods of time; using a variety of ways to collect information; involving children and parents in the assessment process; and issues involved in standardized tests.

Diversity of Backgrounds

The differences of children's backgrounds potentially affects children's progress in learning to read.

Economic Differences   Children's success in school may be influenced by their family's economic background. Children of privilege have many benefits such as numerous outfits of clothes, good nutrition, lots of books and toys, and the latest technology such as T.V.'s, VCRs, computers, and DVDs in their homes. These children probably experience books being read to them and are involved in many family functions and extended activities such as lessons in swimming, skating, music, and the like. They are likely well prepared for the rigors of school. In contrast, at the other end of the socio-economic spectrum, many youngsters come from homes bearing various ills of society such as poverty, abuse, alcoholism, drug abuse, unemployment, and homelessness. Children from these homes are usually less prepared for learning because they frequently get themselves ready for school since both parents may work shifts; they may come to school hungry and sometimes under-nourished; in cold weather they may be inadequately dressed; or they may be under stress because a parent abused them the night before. It is unlikely that many of these children will be ready for the demanding curriculum of the school system. As well, there are millions of American children who don't regularly go to school because they are either homeless or their parents are migrant workers who need their children's help in order to make enough money to eat.

Diversity of Families   The diversity of families may also play a role in many children's progress. Many children come from homes with one parent, or are split between two parents, or live with grandparents or substitute parents. Many of these children may lack structure in their lives and adequate supervision. They may live with high degrees of confusion in their lives and feel insecure, tense, and continually on guard. Many may require special nurturing in order for them to progress successfully.

Differences Between Individual Children   Each individual learner is different from the other: some love art activities more than building with blocks, while others would rather build with Legos and construction toys more than any other activity. Some children prefer to listen to or read books whereas others enjoy running and playing games.

Like adults, children are good at different things: Megan is good at skating; Carlos knows how to climb better than everyone else; Erika can print her name with upper- and lowercase letters, something few other children can do; Raj was able to read before he came to school and spends most of his time in the reading corner; and Majinder is able to write lengthy

143

stories that others can read. You get my point! Children do not progress at the same rate in all subjects all the time. These differences must be taken into account when assessing academic growth.

Developmental Nature of Learning   The developmental nature of learning has many implications for assessment. As mentioned earlier in this book, it is quite natural for some children to become readers earlier than others. Although these differences in progress reflect a normal, developmentally appropriate range of growth, these differences may cause concern for parents. Therefore, when assessing progress of early years children, the nature of developmental learning should be explained to parents. (See Parent Letters 2, 3, 4, and 5.)

Principles of Assessment

Several principles guide assessment practices. They include:

- Assessing while children are engaged in reading;

- Focusing on positive aspects of growth rather than highlighting deficiencies;

- For assessment to be meaningful, it should be conducted over a long period of time; and

- The growth of one child should not be compared to the progress of others.

Assessing in Context   Assessments are more valid and authentic when they are conducted while children are engaged in reading activities. For instance, the only way to assess children's knowledge of books is to watch them hold books up right, turn the pages, and point to words as they look at or read books.

Positive Growth   Young children thrive on praise. So pointing out what they do well is strong motivation to continue to learn. Therefore, note aspects of reading children have accomplished rather than focusing on what they are not yet able to do.

Learning over Time   Single observations provide less information about children's progress than when observations are made several times over the course of a month or two.

Comparing Growth   There is little value in comparing one child's progress to another's, since each child develops in their own unique way.

How one child is developing has little relevance to the growth of another except to develop attitudes of superiority for one at the expense of another.

Assessing Student Growth

Parent Letter 33 helps parents understand some of the philosophical complexities of assessment.

Assessment Instruments

More accurate assessment results when numerous different assessment tools are used: anecdotal records, behavior inventories, work samples, and conferences to name a few.

Anecdotal Records   Anecdotal records are useful for recording information about children's progress. As you notice positive learning behaviors, jot them down. For example, "David pointed to the title of the book and read it; Jean Marc knows the names of books by Robert Munsch; Louise read her sentence strip word for word." Some teachers jot these notes on sticky tab notes they carry around with them for this purpose. Other teachers keep anecdotal record sheets for each subject area pinned onto a clipboard. When they observe some new area of growth, they flip to the subject page and jot down the information into the box reserved for that child. Anecdotal records are easy to make by ruling out a blank page into boxes for each child and labeling each box with a child's name.

Learning Logs   Learning logs are effective for monitoring progress of individual children. They are made from folded cardboard for added strength and then laminated. On each cover, teachers attach a record sheet to track the development of some aspect of language development. On one cover, teachers attach the Emergent reading behavior list and check off the behaviors as children learn them; on another cover, word knowledge is recorded (children list the words they know how to read); on a third cover is a list of initial consonants (teachers circle each letter when children are able to name the letter and identify words that begin with that letter/sound); on an inside cover of the log, children record the names of the stories they have read.

Samples of Work   Another valuable way to assess children's understanding is through samples of work. Paintings, drawings, and sculptures of characters vividly demonstrate what children recall from listening to a story. Similarly, we observe children's comprehension of events in stories when we examine their drawings of key events in a book.

145

Portfolios   Portfolios that reflect samples of best work over time is another effective assessment strategy. Both children and teachers contribute samples of work.

Reading Conferences   Just before a reporting period, many teachers conduct individual student conferences in reading. Children read orally and talk about books while teachers make notes and check off behaviors learned on the Developmental Reading Behavior Inventory in Appendix A. In addition, teachers and students talk about goals and things to work on for the next term.

Involving Parents and Children in Assessment

Both children and parents contribute a great deal to the evaluation process.

Self-Evaluation   Children in the early primary grades (first and second grade) are amazingly aware of their own progress and are able to articulate what they know by telling others, dictating their ideas to an adult, audiotaping information about what they have learned, and writing this information down.

Learning Journals   By the end of the early primary grades (second grade), many children are able to write down what they have learned about their progress in reading, understanding of stories, and ability in speaking and writing.

Parent Assessment   Parents are another source of valuable information about the abilities of children. Ask them to inform you about how they think their child is progressing. Send some guidelines to help them focus their comments: What does your child know about books and authors? In what ways does your child demonstrate interest in books at home? What has your child learned about reading so far this year? What questions do you have about how your child is progressing? The information you receive back from parents will provide many insights into a child's learning. At the same time, you may discover areas in the curricula that require further explanation.

Informing Parents and Caregivers About Assessment Strategies

Parent Letter 34 informs parents about a variety of assessment tools used in classrooms today.

Standardized Tests

Standardized tests are conducted in many early primary classrooms across North America and they are cause for concern in a number of ways.

Decontextualized   The first problem with standardized tests is that they are *not* conducted while children are engaged in reading material of interest to them. Thus, standardized tests cannot determine many early reading behaviors such as book handling, word pointing, or which reading strategies (semantic, syntactic, or graphophonics) children use to figure out unknown words. Moreover, the testing situation is unnatural since teachers cannot provide their usual support when children have difficulty. This causes many youngsters to become tense and anxious.

Test Limited Knowledge   Another concern is that standardized tests examine only a limited number of skills, those that are easily marked by computers. Consequently, phonics skills and word recognition are examined more frequently than children's ability to understand what they read. Processes regarding the strategies children use in reading (semantics, syntax, graphophonics) cannot be evaluated in a standardized test; this kind of crucial information about reading must be observed. Moreover, standardized tests fail to examine children's understanding of characters, events, and problems in stories; nor how they interpret literature (discussion, art, drama); whether their oral responses reflect high level complex thinking; nor their knowledge of many forms of written genre or their knowledge of and appreciation for particular authors. In addition, standardized tests neglect to evaluate children's ability in listening, speaking, and written communication.

Lack of Purpose   Few standardized tests offer any curricular suggestions that might improve a youngster's reading ability. Instead, the test results are used to compare school to school, classroom to classroom, and student to student. Unfortunately, in recent years, test score information has been used in some jurisdictions to determine teachers' salaries and grants from governments for schools. This is especially unfair for schools in low socio-economic areas. As well, standardized tests are used to sort and classify children to determine whether they should progress to the next grade or belong in special classes or gifted programs.

Developmental Nature of Learning   Standardized tests ignore the developmental nature of learning. Therefore, youngsters who are not yet reading words are penalized by the test even though these children may be functioning within developmental benchmarks appropriate for their age.

Objectivity   Another concern regarding standardized tests is their aura of objectivity. Because test scores are often published in newspapers, the public believes that they are a true measure of children's learning.

Trusting Children   Teachers and parents should be mindful of the perils and dangers of standardized tests and limit the detrimental effects they have on children's self-confidence. We need to trust in the children and the authentic assessment procedures used by teachers to provide a more accurate picture of how children grow and develop.

 ### Informing Parents and Care-Givers About Standardized Testing

Standardized testing is discussed in Parent Letter 35. You may copy it and send it home with the children.

COMMUNICATING WITH PARENTS

There are three main types of information important to communicate to parents. First, it's important to inform parents about how instruction is conducted in your classroom; second, parents want to know how their children are progressing and third, what they can do to support their learning.

Sharing Curricular Information

There are several ways to inform parents about how instruction is conducted in your classroom. Following are some ideas.

Curricula Nights   Early in the school year is an ideal time to invite parents to an evening in your classroom to discuss teaching and learning.

• *Characteristics of Young Children.* During a curricula night is also a good time to talk about the nature of young children and their need for physical activity as well as stimulating and thought-provoking learning activities. Refer to Parent Letters 1 and 2, which outline the nature of young learners.

• *Goals.* Discuss your overall goals for developing literacy in your classroom and share your philosophy of teaching and learning. Also, ask parents to jot down their goals for their children and have them share these with the whole group. Collect parents' goals and note the extent to which their goals are consistent with yours. Some parent goals may be topics for future parent meetings and newsletters.

• *Value of Reading Good Literature.* Talk about the value of reading good literature to children and read them a selection the class particularly enjoys. Encourage parents to take their children to the public library regularly and to read to their children on a daily basis (see Parent Letters 13, 14, and 15).

• *Value of Center Activities.* Walk around your classroom and talk about what is learned in each activity center and share samples of work completed by their children (see Parent Letter 9).

• *Questions and Answers.* Leave a good amount of time for a question and answer session. Ask someone to take notes so that you can follow up on some of their questions and concerns through newsletters. A good way to end a curricula evening is by giving parents a curricular handbook outlining your plans for the next month or term.

Curricular Outlines   Many teachers develop curricular handbooks for parents, outlining their language arts programs including strategies used, daily timetables, and activities parents can do at home with their children to develop literacy. Refer to the Parent Letters and select several letters to include in your curricular outlines. These letters may be duplicated for your convenience.

Multimedia Presentations   Once your classroom is up and running, consider taking slides or video of the children engaged in various activities such as reading aloud, a shared reading session, and center activities. Have a special night devoted just to watching these pictures and discussing what is learned during these activities.

Newsletters   Parents enjoy weekly or monthly newsletters that inform them about what is going on in your classroom, the topics you're studying, and the books you're reading. Newsletters can also be used to make specific requests for learning materials ("We need used computer paper for the art center") and to inform them of special events ("Picture day is Thursday, October 15"). The newsletter is also a vehicle for celebrating successes of children ("Today Markus dictated a story 15 sentences long").

Curricular Newsletters   Some newsletters are devoted solely to curricular issues such as how you use literature in the classroom; the value of dictated stories; strategies that develop successful readers. The curricular newsletter also provides opportunities to review specific ways parents can support literacy at home: how to read effectively to children, how to develop word knowledge naturally, and how to use phonics in meaningful ways. The many Parent Letters referred to throughout this book can be included in parent newsletters. You are welcome to copy them for this purpose.

Parent Volunteers   One of the best ways to inform parents about your language arts program is to ask them to volunteer in your classroom. Once they have taken dictation from youngsters, read stories to them, listened to them read and write, set-up art centers, they will have a much better understanding of how children learn in your classroom.

Learning Kits   Another effective way to inform parents about curricula is to get them involved with helping their children further develop literacy. Teachers frequently develop learning kits to send home that include materials such as literature selections as well as procedures for various reading activities. The parent letters referred to in this book can be made into learning kits very easily.

Communicating Children's Progress

Bobbi Fisher (1995) maintains that there are two important messages parents want to hear: recognition of their children's efforts, and celebration of their successes. Celebrating children's accomplishments takes time, but parents will love you for the effort.

Good News Newsletters   Several times a year, devote newsletters to the good things the children in your class have accomplished. Some of the news is written by you, but youngsters can also write about things they have learned or they can dictate stories about one of their special accomplishments.

Good Work Certificates   Send home good work certificates as often as you can. Have the children themselves write the note and you sign it.

Telephone Calls/E-Mail   Invite children to telephone or e-mail their parents to tell them how well they told a story; how they painted a picture of a character in a story; or how well they read a pattern book all by themselves.

Class Photo Album   Take pictures of children celebrating their good work, put the pictures into a class album, and invite children to write the captions or dictate stories to accompany each picture.

Parent-Teacher Dialogue Journals   An idea Bobbi Fisher (1991) suggests is to develop dialogue journals with parents. In each parent dialogue journal, she writes short descriptions of something positive about each child and asks parents to respond by sharing positive things their children are doing at home. The dialogue journal provides a wonderful opportunity for parents to ask questions about what is happening at school.

Parent Conferences   In most schools teachers are required to have conferences with individual parents twice a year. Many teachers have these conferences with children present. In fact, children are very adept at explaining to their parents about what they are learning. These conferences begin by sharing the positive progress children are making and parents too are asked to contribute positive things their children are doing at home. Then teachers discuss growth over time and things they and the children will be working on during the next term. Children also share their goals and accomplishments. Ways parents can support growth is also discussed.

Informing Parents About Building Effective Communication Between Home and School

Parent Letter 36 discusses ways parents can build communication with the school.

It has been my goal to share the techniques and strategies that teach young children to learn and grow as readers. The early years are crucial for developing a love of reading, and it is my hope the strategies covered in this book will foster this lifelong passion for reading.

Appendix A: Developmental Reading Behavior Inventory

EMERGENT READING PHASE

In the Emergent phase, children become interested in books and enjoy hearing stories read to them. Children in the Emergent phase do not attend to individual words and yet they learn so much about literacy including comprehension and concepts about books. They demonstrate many early reading behaviors and begin to employ reading strategies. Following are specific behaviors associated with the Emergent phase.

Behaviors

Many of these behaviors are observed as children respond to books after they hear stories read aloud to them. Other behaviors are noted as children handle books themselves.

1. Comprehension

   The Child

   ▶ enjoys listening to stories being read to them;
   ▶ predicts what may happen in stories based on information on the cover;
   ▶ selects books for adults to read to them;
   ▶ chooses to have the same book read over and over again;
   ▶ makes sound effects for objects and animals in stories they hear;
   ▶ discusses pictures in books as they are read to them;
   ▶ relates events in stories to personal experiences;
   ▶ recalls some details from stories that have been read to them;
   ▶ recalls details, events, and main ideas in stories that are read to them;
   ▶ recognizes some elements in stories (characters and events);
   ▶ recognizes that print in books remains the same and will tell adults if they miss words, sentences, and pages when reading aloud;

▶ interprets stories that have been read to them through discussion, art, and drama.

2. Concepts of Print Material

The Child

▶ recognizes books written by the same author;

▶ recognizes books written by a few different authors;

▶ names a few authors of predictable books;

▶ recognizes some ways print material is organized (genre) such as predictable pattern literature, chart stories, and poetry.

3. Reading Behaviors

The Child

▶ chooses to look at books independently;

▶ retells stories by looking at illustrations;

▶ retells familiar predictable stories in sequence;

▶ holds books right side up;

▶ turns pages in books in an appropriate order;

▶ knows that the black marks on the page carry a message;

▶ understands that print starts at the top of the page and ends at the bottom of the page;

▶ understands that print goes left to right across the page;

▶ follows along with the 'reading' of predictable repeated lines and refrains in text;

▶ recalls repeated phrases, sentences, and refrains accurately;

▶ retells familiar stories with much accuracy (appears to have memorized the story).

4. Word Knowledge

The Child

▶ points to clumps of letters and assigns oral responses;

▶ points to words in a left-to-right motion in repeated phrases, sentences, and refrains in familiar predictable pattern stories;

▶ matches word cards to same words in dictated sentences;

▶ matches words to those same words in familiar phrases and sentences (sentence strips);

▶ recognizes their name in print and familiar names of friends;

▶ recognizes print in their environment (stop signs, names around the classroom and school);

> ▶ points to a few familiar words in stories;
> ▶ identifies approximately ten individual words in familiar predictable pattern books, charts, or Big Books.

5. Reading Strategies

The Child

> ▶ uses semantics (pictures and memory of stories) when 'reading' alone;
> ▶ uses syntax (repeated lines and refrains) to assist them with their reading;
> ▶ can give an oral retelling that is often very similar to the print in the text.

BEGINNING READING PHASE

Children in the Beginning phase extend their ability in comprehending stories, concepts of books, knowledge of words, and ability in employing reading strategies. By the end of the Beginning phase children are able to read independently about ten familiar sentence strips, about five predictable pattern selections, and recognize approximately 30 individual words.

Beginning Phase Behaviors

Following are specific behaviors children might demonstrate in the Beginning phase of reading.

1. Comprehension (as they listen to books being read to them)

The Child

> ▶ continues to enjoy hearing stories read to them;
> ▶ continues to predict what stories will be about by examining covers;
> ▶ continues to recall details, events, main ideas, and problems in stories;
> ▶ continues to relate events in stories to personal experiences;
> ▶ understands elements of stories (characters, events, endings) in stories they hear;
> ▶ retells stories they have heard in logical order;
> ▶ gains deeper meanings from stories that are read to them;
> ▶ interprets stories they hear through discussions, art, and drama.

2. Concepts of Print Material

The Child

- recognizes several ways written material is organized (genre) such as pattern books, complex picture books, poetry, and nonfiction;
- recognizes books by titles and authors;
- understands what authors and illustrators do;
- becomes familiar with several different authors.

3. Reading Behaviors

The Child

- chooses to look at books and tries to read them;
- points to words and assigns an oral response for each word;
- points to text in a left-to-right direction across pages;
- points to individual words on repeated lines and refrains in familiar predictable pattern stories;
- points to words and reads accurately repeated lines and refrains in familiar predictable pattern stories;
- points to words and reads words accurately in up to five dictated sentence strips;
- points to words and reads accurately about five familiar predictable pattern stories.

4. Word Knowledge

The Child

- points to words and assigns a meaningful oral response;
- matches word cards to same words in dictated sentence strips;
- reads words in the environment such as signs and labels around the classroom and school;
- recognizes about 30 different individual words in familiar contexts (predictable pattern selections, sentence strips, charts, Big Books, and signs).

5. Reading Strategies

The Child

- uses semantics (pictures, meaning, background experiences, memory) to get meaning from text;
- uses syntax (repeated words, phrases, sentences, and refrains) to gain meaning while reading;
- sometimes guesses at words in order to retain meaning.

DEVELOPING READING PHASE

During the Developing phase of reading children begin to comprehend at deeper levels, understand concepts of books, recognize many words in familiar reading material, and employ more reading strategies. By the end of the Developing phase, children are able to read independently about ten familiar pattern selections and about 15 sentence strips, and recognize about 50 different words.

Developing Reading Behaviors

Specific behaviors at the Developing phase are outlined below.

1. Comprehension (as the child listens to stories)

   The Child

   ▶ continues to understand how stories relate to their experiences;
   ▶ continues to predict what stories will be about from examining covers;
   ▶ understands more story elements (characters, events, problems, endings) from stories they hear;
   ▶ recalls details, main ideas, characters, events, and problems in stories they hear;
   ▶ interprets stories through drama, art, discussion, book talks, dictation.

2. Concepts of Print Material

   The Child

   ▶ recognizes several ways print material is organized (genre) such as pattern books, picture books, poetry, charts, lists, and nonfiction;
   ▶ recognizes several familiar authors;
   ▶ chooses books by title or favorite authors;
   ▶ reads titles and page numbers in books;
   ▶ recognizes authors, titles, and illustrators of many familiar books.

3. Reading Behaviors

   The Child

   ▶ chooses to read books as a self-initiated activity;
   ▶ reads aloud in a way that conveys meaning (retells familiar stories);
   ▶ reads familiar material first (sentence strips, predictable pattern literature, chart stories, Big Books);

▶ reads word-by-word familiar sentence strips they have dictated;

▶ reads independently about 15 sentence strips;

▶ reads slowly and laboriously at first;

▶ reads word-by-word familiar pattern selections with assistance;

▶ reads word-by-word familiar pattern selections independently;

▶ reads independently about 10 familiar pattern selections;

▶ reads current dictated story with assistance;

▶ reads current dictated story independently;

▶ follows simple written instructions.

4. Word Knowledge

The Child

▶ recognizes words in many familiar contexts (in the environment, chart stories, sentence strips, predictable pattern literature, Big Books, dictated stories);

▶ recognizes about 50 different words from familiar contexts;

▶ sorts words according to action, objects, color, animals, etc.;

▶ creates sentences from known word cards.

5. Reading Strategies

The Child

▶ uses semantics (context, pictures, memory, experiences) to get meaning from print material;

▶ uses syntax (word and sentence patterns, refrains) to assist reading;

▶ uses phonics (initial consonants) to gain meaning from text;

▶ guesses words that make sense in the text;

▶ self-corrects when word chosen doesn't make sense;

▶ uses punctuation to guide oral reading (periods, question marks);

▶ recognizes initial consonants in familiar words;

▶ recognizes final consonants in familiar words.

INDEPENDENT READING PHASE

At the Independent phase of reading children understand literature at a more complex level while using listening materials and also understand what they read for themselves. As well, they begin to read both familiar and unfamiliar material. By the end of this phase children can read about 20 familiar pattern selections, about 10 unfamiliar pattern selections, their own dictated stories, and recognize about 100 different words.

Independent Reading Phase Behaviors

Specific behaviors of the Independent phase are listed below.

1. Comprehension (while listening to material read to them)

   The Child

   ▶ understands story structures (characters, events, problems, solutions) from stories they hear;

   ▶ predicts what stories will be about by examining covers and changes predictions based on new information;

   ▶ recalls many details, main ideas, problems, events in stories they hear;

   ▶ interprets stories they hear and read through art, drama, discussion, book talks, dictated responses, and written responses.

2. Concepts of Print Material

   The Child

   ▶ recognizes many ways written materials are organized (genre) such as predictable pattern books, complex picture books, charts, poetry, nonfiction, letters, fantasy;

   ▶ identifies works from numerous authors and chooses to read particular authors;

   ▶ identifies characteristics of particular authors;

   ▶ selects books by title, author, and subject of interest;

   ▶ recognizes book titles and page numbers.

3. Reading Behaviors

   The Child

   ▶ reads many familiar predictable pattern selections independently;

   ▶ reads independently familiar poetry, Big Books, chart stories, lists, sentence strips;

   ▶ reads aloud familiar print fluently;

   ▶ reads about 20 familiar predictable pattern selections;

   ▶ reads about 10 unfamiliar predictable pattern selections;

   ▶ reads unfamiliar predictable pattern literature in guided reading sessions;

   ▶ reads unfamiliar text in a word-by-word fashion, slowly and deliberately;

   ▶ reads unfamiliar text with greater fluency;

> reads current dictated stories with assistance;
> reads current dictated stories independently;
> reads published dictated stories fluently;
> reads aloud in a way that conveys meaning (fluently and with expression);
> follows written instructions;
> chooses to read as a self-initiated activity.

4. Word Knowledge

The Child

> sorts words in a variety of ways (animals, people, homes, action words, etc.);
> sorts words according to word families (*can, fan, ban, tan, man*);
> creates rhyming families (*red, fed, Ted, bed*);
> creates new sentences from known word cards;
> identifies about 100 different words from familiar contexts.

5. Reading Strategies

The Child

> uses semantics (context, pictures, memory, experiences) to get meaning from text;
> uses syntax (word and sentence patterns, refrains) to assist reading;
> uses phonics to predict meaning of words (consonants, word families);
> guesses for words in order to retain meaning;
> self-corrects in order to retain meaning;
> uses punctuation to guide oral reading (periods, question marks, and commas).

Appendix B: Story to Be Used with Developmental Reading Test in Chapter One

MARMALADE CAT

Early one morning Marmalade Cat went for a
walk with his momma.
On the way he saw a yellow butterfly.
"Look at the yellow butterfly!" called Marmalade
Cat.
"Hurry up. Hurry up. Don't be slow.
Hurry up, Hurry up. We have to go," called
Momma Cat.
So on they went.

Then Marmalade Cat saw a green duck.
"Look at the green duck!" called Marmalade Cat.
"Hurry up. Hurry up. Don't be slow.
Hurry up, Hurry up. We have to go," called
Momma Cat.
So on they went.

Then Marmalade Cat saw a brown dog.
"Look at the brown dog!" called Marmalade Cat.
"Hurry up. Hurry up. Don't be slow.
Hurry up, Hurry up. We have to go," called
Momma Cat.
So on they went.

Then Marmalade Cat saw a gray mouse.
"Hurry up. Hurry up. Don't be slow!
Hurry up. Hurry up. We have to go!" called Mar-
malade Cat.
"Let's catch him!"

—Gail Heald-Taylor

Appendix C: Glossary

. . . .

The following definitions are a synthesis of several authors and bodies of work (Heald-Taylor, 1987, 1989; Moustafa, 1996; Tompkins, Pollard, Bright, & Winsor, 1999; Tompkins, 1998; Savage, 1998; IRA & NCTE, 1996; Weaver, 1994).

Approximate Spelling: See *Spelling*

Assessment Tools: Assessment tools are formats for collecting information about children's progress in reading. Assessment tools may include anecdotal records, learning logs, portfolios, learning journals, and self-evaluation.

Author Studies: During author studies, children read and respond to stories written by a particular author. As well, children examine the books by an author to determine characteristics of their style. Children also read information about the author, write letters to the author, and if possible, invite the author to visit their school.

Beginning Reading: In this handbook, Beginning reading refers to a phase of reading where children begin to understand how print works: that it moves across the page in a left-to-right direction and from the top to bottom of the page, and that pages are turned from left to right. As well, children in this phase begin to recognize some repeated pattern sentences and individual words in the stories they read.

Big Books: These are predictable pattern selections in an oversized format that contain enlarged print. In this handbook we talk about making class Big Books with text from predictable pattern selections printed at the top of each page and the rest of the page left blank for the children to illustrate the text. There are several types of class-made Big Books: 1) a replica book— an exact copy of a predictable pattern selection; 2) newly illustrated books—a familiar book with new illustrations; 3) adapted book—a new version of a predictable pattern selection; and 4) an original Big Book—an original book composed by the children dictating the story.

Book Share: See *Book Talk*

Book Talks: One way children review books they have read is by giving a talk about the book with a peer, small group, or with the whole class. During the book talk (book share), children name the title, author, and illustrator and tell a small portion of the book to entice others to read it. At the end of a book talk, peers usually ask the presenters questions about the book.

Chart Stories: These are developed when groups of children contribute to the composition of a story or information piece. Each child's contribution to the piece is usually limited to a single sentence.

Cloze Procedure: Cloze involves deleting words from text and requiring the reader to fill in the missing words. This is a useful strategy for Emergent and Beginning readers to help them identify words in familiar text and to use the context of the text to figure out the meaning.

Complex Picture Books: Compared to predictable pattern literature, complex picture books have more complex story structures, more words per page, illustrations that expand the text rather than corresponding to it, individual sentences are longer and more complex, print font size is smaller, and more background information is required to comprehend these books.

Comprehension: This is a term used to describe the interpretations, understanding, and meaning readers construct as they listen to and read stories.

Concept Books: These books focus on dimensions of an object or abstract idea to develop understanding. Concept books discuss such things as color, counting, size, shape, or opposites. Many concept books focus on language such as letters of the alphabet, prepositions (*in, on, around*), nouns, verbs, and descriptive words.

Consonants: These are all the letters in the alphabet other than vowels.

Beginning Consonants: These are the consonants that are placed at the beginning of words.

Cursive Writing: In this style of writing, each letter in a word is connected to the previous letter. Adults generally use cursive writing when they write notes, messages, and handwritten correspondence.

Developmental Phases of Reading: Although children do not necessarily proceed through set stages of development, there is substantial research evidence suggesting that there are recurring patterns of early children's reading experiences. The developmental phases described in this handbook reflect these observations of early reading behaviors reported in the research literature.

Developing Phase of Reading: This term is used in this handbook to describe several abilities of young readers including understanding of complex picture books that are read to them, recognition of authors and their style of writing, understanding of parts of books (titles, illustrators, dedications) and different genres. Children in the Developing phase also begin to read familiar rehearsed predictable pattern selections, chart stories, and sentence strips. As well, by the end of this phase children recognize many individual words and begin to identify the initial and final sounds in familiar words.

Dialogue Journals: Parent-teacher dialogue journals, suggested by Bobbi Fisher (1991), are notebooks that travel between the teacher and the parent where each writes notes to the other regarding such topics as positive abilities of children, how children are progressing, questions parents have about school, response to what children are learning, and so on.

Dictated Sentence: See *Sentence Strips*

Dictated Story: This is an oral composition several sentences long that an individual child tells while an adult records it in manuscript print. In this process the child concentrates on the composing and telling while the adult addresses spelling and grammar issues.

Directionality: This is the left-to-right direction that print moves across the page and the left-to-right direction pages are turned in books.

Early Primary Children: This term is used in this handbook to refer to children attending school in kindergarten to second grade.

Early Years Children: This term refers to youngsters in the preschool years during the ages of one to four.

Emergent Reading: This is a common term in the research literature that refers to the development of the association of print with meaning that begins early in a child's life and continues until the child reaches the stage of conventional reading and writing (IRA & NCTE, 1996). In this handbook, the Emergent phase refers to several specific reading behaviors. During this phase children enjoy hearing stories being read to them; they begin to recognize how print works, that it has a left-to-right direction, and that pages are turned in a left-to-right direction; they begin to retell familiar predictable pattern selections but they do not usually attend to the actual print. However, by the end of this phase, children begin to recognize a few words in familiar contexts.

Fine Motor Dexterity: This refers to small muscle coordination in young children affecting their ability to grasp and manipulate pencils, paint brushes, crayons, and scissors. Fine muscles are not fully developed in early years and early primary children.

Flannel Board: This is a type of story board on which children make visual cut-outs of the story elements and place them on a large board covered with flannel fabric.

Focus Question: This is a broad question that is asked before reading aloud a selection to children in order to help young learners focus their attention while listening to the story.

Framing: Words are framed when the index finger on the left hand points to the beginning of a word and the index finger on the right hand points to the end of a word.

Genre: This refers to a particular category of literature. Varieties of genre useful for young children include predictable pattern literature, folktales, refrain books, complex picture books, issue books, poetry, nonfiction (informational books), dictated stories, and chart stories.

Guided Reading: During the assisted reading process, children attempt to read familiar, rehearsed selections independently while teachers provide assistance when required. During this process, teachers read the selection to the children, teachers and children read the selection together, children re-read the selection in unison before individual children attempt to read the selection alone. Teachers provide assistance during each phase.

Independent Reading: Children read independently when they read silently by themselves at their own pace with books they have chosen that interest them and are at their reading level. In this handbook, Independent reading also refers to a specific set of reading behaviors associated with the Independent phase of reading development as well as instructional strategies that enable children to become independent readers. At the Independent phase, children begin to read both familiar and unfamiliar predictable texts and refrain books. They are able to recognize more than one hundred words and begin to employ many reading strategies such as semantics, syntax, and graphophonics.

Integrated Reading Strategies: Children integrate reading strategies when they employ several different strategies to gain meaning from text. These include *semantics* (background knowledge of the topic, pictures, memory from a previous reading); *context clues* (information presented in the surrounding passage that helps the reader gain meaning); *syntax* (the general order and pattern of language as well as grammatical function of words); and *graphophonics* (using knowledge of sound/symbol relationships).

Isolated Skill Instruction: See *Skill Instruction*

Issue Books: These are a type of complex picture book that deals with issues in children's lives, their community, and society. Issue books also deal with social justice issues such as name calling, bullying, racial prejudice, gender, preserving the environment, cruelty to animals, death, homelessness, and poverty.

Learning Centers: In learning centers children sometimes work alone, with partners, or collaboratively in groups to interpret the literature they read and to reinforce their listening, speaking, writing, and reading abilities. Language learning centers involve listening, speaking, drama, art, dictated stories, writing, word study, and reading books.

Letter Recognition: This occurs when children are able to identify and name letters of the alphabet.

Listening Level Comprehension: Young children are able to *listen to* and understand more complex text than they are able to independently read and understand themselves.

Literacy: According to *Standards for the English Language Arts* (IRA & NCTE, 1996), "literacy involves the capacity to accomplish a wide range of reading, writing, speaking, and other language tasks associated with everyday life" (p. 73). This handbook deals mainly with reading strategies.

Literary Activities: Literary activities are those activities that extend and expand ability in listening, speaking, reading, and writing.

Manuscript Print: This is a type of print where each letter stands alone and is unconnected to letters adjacent to it. Manuscript print is used in type-written text, in books, and is the type of print that teachers use on chart stories in the classroom.

Meaningful Print: See *Print*

Mobile: This is a visual representation of story elements in stories that are cut from paper and hung by string from a dowel or coat hanger.

Nonfiction: Nonfiction is a term used for reading material with a predominance of information in it.

Over-Copying: Young children increase fine muscle coordination when they copy over each letter in words in sentences that have been printed in manuscript by the teacher on long strips of paper called sentence strips.

Phonics: This is one of the cueing systems readers use to read and write. Phonics refers to the system of sound/letter relationships beginning with the understanding that each letter of the English alphabet stands for one or more sounds (IRA & NCTE, 1996).

Phonetically Regular Text: This type of text is limited to words and word parts that are easily decodable according to phonic principles that have been previously taught. Phonetically regular text often employs words that have consistent sound/symbol relationships and can often result in stories with short choppy sentences and uninteresting story lines.

Predictable Pattern Literature: In this literature the language in the stories is usually familiar to the children, there are often only a few words on each page, some sentences and phrases are repeated several times in the story, and stories frequently have a strong rhythm and rhyme. Illustrations in predictable pattern literature are large, vivid, and colorful. The illustrations alone represent the story told by the print. All these features enable children to anticipate and predict the next sentence or episode in the story.

Rehearsed Predictable Pattern Literature: This refers to predictable pattern selections children have heard previously and have read over and over with the teacher, in unison and alone.

Predicting: This is a reading strategy children use to anticipate what will happen next in stories. These predictions (guesses) are based on children's knowledge of the topic, information in the text, and the illustrations.

Print Awareness: This is a term used for children who begin to notice the direction that print moves on a page, spaces between words, and begin to recognize signs, labels, and letters in their environment and in books.

Print Text: Any text that creates meaning through writing, such as stories, poems, notes, and letters is called print text (*Standards for the English Language Arts* 1996, p. 74).

Meaningful Print: Meaningful print is text that employs interesting language, engaging story lines, and provokes thoughtful reflection.

Prompting Questions: Questions teachers ask children in order to extend their thinking after listening to a literature selection are called prompting questions. Prompting questions are also used to help children extend their personal dictated stories and written compositions.

Read-Aloud Sessions: In this handbook, this is a term used to describe ways adults read to children. During read-aloud sessions adults introduce children to authors, illustrators, and ways to interpret stories in order to develop understanding and comprehension.

Reading Behavior Inventory: A reading behavior inventory is a list of reading behaviors children demonstrate as they listen to, look at, and read text.

The reading behaviors listed in the Developmental Reading Behavior Inventory (Appendix A) in this handbook are organized into four phases indicating different benchmarks of behaviors.

Reading Log: This is a form children fill out indicating the books they have read and the date they read them.

Refrain Books: These are a type of literature that incorporates a repeated stanza chorus or refrain throughout the piece. For the most part, refrain books have more dense print on each page and fewer pictures than predictable pattern literature. Two types of refrain books are described in this handbook. The first type is called *easy-read* refrain books and the second is called *traditional* refrain books. Easy-read refrain books have less dense print on each page and more illustrations in the selection than traditional refrain books. In addition to the repeated refrain, traditional refrain books usually have more complex story structures than easy-read refrain books. Compared to easy-read refrain books, traditional refrain books have some unique features: characters are usually animals that come in sets of three (The Three Bears, The Three Little Pigs, The Three Billy Goats Gruff), characters are mainly good or bad, and there are frequently three episodes in the story.

Regular Spelling: See *Spelling*

Response Journal: This is a notebook where children write about what they thought about the books they heard read to them or they have read themselves.

Retelling: This occurs when children orally recall a story that has been read to them.

Self-Correcting: When children self-correct, they correct mistakes they made while reading a passage.

Semantics: This is one of the cueing systems readers use to construct meaning in text. The semantic system focuses on the meaning of texts, where meaning is seen as connections between words, and the reader's prior knowledge of language, understanding of the world, and experience of other texts (IRA & NCTE, 1996).

Sentence Strips: This is a sentence that is written down on a strip of paper 6″ × 18″. The adult prints the sentence using manuscript print (text used in books) rather than cursive writing, the type of print adults use for their personal writing. Sentences are usually dictated by the children reflecting personal experiences (dictated sentence), although sentence strips are also made from repeated lines and phrases in predictable pattern literature. Sentence strips are used to draw attention to sentences, words, letters, and phonics.

Shared Reading: In the shared reading process, developed by Don Holdaway (1979), teachers use predictable pattern literature in over-sized books with enlarged print for reading instruction. In this process the teacher reads the predictable pattern literature to the children and invites them to read along when they can. Children then read the selection together in unison several times before individual children read the selection alone. After each re-reading, children participate in activities in order to develop and extend understanding of the story through art, drama, and writing activities. As well, the predictable pattern story becomes the basis for examining sentences, words, and phonics.

Skill Instruction: There are two types of skill instruction described in this handbook, direct skill instruction and contextual skill instruction.

Isolated Skill Instruction: During this type of instruction, teachers formally teach skills such as phonics, grammar, and spelling as separate discreet subjects with no connection to children's reading material or their writing.

Contextual Skill Instruction: During contextual skill instruction, phonics skills are taught with the language in literature selections and with words children already know. In this way, children make analogies between familiar and unfamiliar print. For example, when children recognize the word *black* in a story they have heard, read with others, and read alone, they are in a better position to be able to understand unknown words with the same rime *ack* such as *back, rack, stack, tack*. Similarly, children's writing provides the vehicle (context) for instruction in spelling and grammar.

Sound/Symbol Relationships: When children attempt to make an oral sound to correspond to a letter symbol, they are making a sound/symbol relationship. Some sound/symbol relationships are generalizable, that is, certain letters consistently represent the same sound such as the consonants *b, d, f, j, l, m, n, p, q, r, v, w,* and *z*. Other letters do not always represent a consistent sound such as the letter *c*, which sometimes has an *s* sound and other times represents a *k* sound.

Spelling: Two types of spelling are described in this book, approximate spelling and standard spelling.

Approximate Spelling: This is a term used to refer to nonstandard spelling young children use in their personal story writing based mainly on their knowledge of phonics, the relationship between phonology (the sounds in speech), and letters of the alphabet. Children rely mainly on their speech and understanding of letters in the alphabet to guide their spelling. Children using approximate spellings may write the sentence, "I like playing with my friends because they're fun." like this, *I lik pla w mi freds becuz thr fun.* Other terms used for approximate spellings are phonetic spelling, developmental spelling, invented spelling, and temporary spelling.

Regular Spelling: See *Standard Spelling*

Standard Spelling: According to Margaret Moustafa (1997), standard spelling is a set of arbitrary, socially agreed upon conventions specific to each word (p. 87). Thus the word *cat* in the English speaking world is spelled *cat* and not as *catt, catte, kat, katt,* or *katte* as it was during the seventeenth century (Moustafa, 1996).

Story Map: This is a visual representation of the plot, events, characters, problems, and ending of stories. Children paint or draw these representations.

Story Structures: The elements of story structures include characters, plots, problems, events, setting, point of view, endings, and other elements that make stories complex and interesting (Tompkins, 1998).

Syntax: This is one of the cueing systems readers use to construct meaning in text. The syntactic system focuses on the relationship among linguistic units such as prefixes, suffixes, words, phrases, and clauses. Syntax also refers to the pattern or structure of word order in sentences, clauses, and phrases (IRA & NCTE, 1996).

Tandem Reading: When children and adults read in tandem, the child reads while the teacher fades in and out to maintain the fluency of the reading.

Text: This refers to all reading material, literature, dictated stories, chart stories, signs in the environment, and so on.

Theme Studies: These are units of study that focus on one topic and integrate reading, writing, listening, and speaking. Theme studies often integrate other curricular disciplines such as mathematics, science, and social studies. During theme studies children explore many types of literature including predictable pattern literature, complex picture books, informational text, poetry, and song.

Under-Copying: Children develop fine muscle control and handwriting skill when they copy under each letter in words in a sentence that teachers print onto long strips of paper called sentence strips.

Venn Diagram: This is a format for organizing information about different objects. For example, when recording information about chickens and ducks, on one section of the Venn diagram characteristics about chickens are listed, in another section of the Venn diagram, characteristics of ducks are recorded, and in a third intersection of the Venn diagram is listed information common to both chickens and ducks.

Word Families: In this handbook, word families are words that have common rimes. For example, the words *black, pack, Jack,* and *rack* have a common rime "ack." Children enjoy making word families from other common rimes when they occur in the material they read. Common rimes include *ake, ame, ap, at, ate, aw, ill, in, ock, ug, un.*

Wordless Books: These are books that represent an entire story through illustrations. The absence of words allows children to focus their whole attention on the illustrations to communicate the story rather than words.

Appendix D: Literature Selections for Literacy Activities

. . . .

WORDLESS BOOKS

Ahlberg, A. & C. McNaughton. 1984. *Zoo*. London: Dragon Books.

Alexander, M. 1970. *Bobo's Dream*. New York: Dial.

Aliki. 1995. *Tabby: A Story in Pictures*. New York: Harper Collins.

Anno, M. 1977. *Anno's Journey*. New York: Collins.

Aruego, J. 1971. *Look What I Can Do*. New York: Charles Scribner's Sons.

Boynton, S. 1980. *If at First . . .* Boston: Little Brown and Company.

Briggs, R. 1978. *The Snowman*. New York: Random House.

———. 1985. *Building the Snowman*. New York: Little Brown.

Brinckloe, J. 1974. *The Spider Web*. Garden City, New York: Doubleday.

Carle, E. 1971. *Do You Want to Be My Friend?* New York: Collins.

Day, A. 1985. *Good Dog Carl*. San Marcos, CA: Green Tiger Press.

———. 1990. *Carl's Christmas*. New York: Farrar, Straus & Giroux.

de Paola, T. 1978. *Pancakes for Breakfast*. New York: Harcourt, Brace Jovanovich.

Drescher, H. 1987. *The Yellow Umbrella*. New York: Bradbury.

Florian, D. 1984. *Airplane Ride*. New York: Crowell.

Goodall, J. 1975. *Creepy Castle*. New York: Macmillan Publishers Ltd.

Hoban, T. 1978. *Is It Red? Is It Yellow? Is It Blue?* New York: Greenwillow.

———. 1981. *Take Another Look*. New York: Greenwillow.

———. 1983. *I Read Signs*. New York: Greenwillow.

Hutchins, P. 1971. *Changes, Changes*. New York: Macmillan.

Kilbourne, F. 1977. *Overnight Adventure*. Toronto: The Women's Press.

Lisker, S. 1975. *Lost*. New York: Harcourt, Brace Jovanovich.

Mari, I. & E. Mari, 1969. *The Apple and the Moth*. New York: Pantheon.

Mayer, M. 1973. *Bubble, Bubble*. New York: Parents' Magazine.

———. 1974. *Frog Goes to Dinner*. New York: Dial.

———. 1975. *One Frog Too Many*. New York: Dial.

Mayer, M. & Marianna Mayer, 1971. *A Boy, a Dog, a Frog and a Friend*. New York: Dial.

McCully, E.M. 1984. *Picnic*. New York: Harper & Row.

———. 1985. *First Snow*. New York: Harper & Row.

———. 1988. *New Baby*. New York: Harper & Row.

Omerod, J. 1981. *Sunlight*. New York: Lothrop.

———. 1982. *Moonlight*. New York: Lothrop.

Spier, P. 1977. *Noah's Arc*. New York: Doubleday.

Turkle, B. 1976. *Deep in the Forest*. New York: Dutton.

Ueno, N. 1973. *Elephant Buttons*. New York: Harper & Row.

Wiesner, D. 1991. *Tuesday*. New York: Clarion.

Willard, N. 1977. *Simple Pictures Are Best*. New York: Harcourt, Brace Jovanovich.

Winter, P. 1976. *The Bear and the Fly*. New York: Crown.

REPETITION PREDICTABLE PATTERN BOOKS

Asch, F. 1985. *I Can Roar*. Toronto: Kids Can Press.

———. 1997. *I Can Blink*. Toronto: Kids Can Press.

Campbell, R. 1985. *Dear Zoo*. New York: Viking Penguin.

Carle, E. 1997. *From Head to Toe*. New York: Scholastic.

———. 2000. *Does a Kangaroo Have a Mother, Too?* New York: Harper Collins.

Chang, C. 1996. *Are You My Baby?* New York: Intervisual Books and Random House.

Christelow, E. 1989. *Five Little Monkeys Jumping on the Bed*. New York: Scholastic Inc.

de Paola, T. 1980. *If He's My Brother*. Englewood Cliffs, NJ: Prentice-Hall, Inc.

Ginsburg, M. 1972. *The Chick and the Duckling*. New York: Aladdin Books, Macmillan Publishing.

Hutchins, P. 1972. *Good Night Owl!* New York: Macmillan Publishing Co.

Kraus, R. 2000. *Whose Mouse Are You?* New York: Simon & Schuster.

Lacome, J. 1992. *Noisy Noises on the Farm*. London: Walker Books.

London, J. 1999. *Wiggle Waggle*. San Diego: Harcourt Brace & Company.

———. 2000. *Snuggle Wuggle*. San Diego: Harcourt Brace & Company.

Martin, B. Jr. 1991. *Polar Bear, Polar Bear, What Do You Hear?* New York: Henry Holt & Company.

———. 1992. *Brown Bear, Brown Bear, What Do You See?* New York: Henry Holt & Company.

———. 1999. *A Beasty Story*. New York: Harcourt Brace & Company.

Pandell, K. 1994. *I love You, Sun. I Love You, Moon*. New York: Putnam's Sons.

Tafuri, N. 1985. *Have You Seen My Duckling?* New York: Greenwillow.

———. 1997. *What the Sun Sees: What the Moon Sees*. New York: Scholastic.

Watanabe, S. 1982. *I Can Ride It!* New York: Philomel Books: Putnam Publishing.

———. 1984. *How Do I Put It On?* New York: Penguin Books.

Weiss, N. 1990. *Where Does the Brown Bear Go?* New York: Puffin Books, The Penguin Group.

Wildsmith, B. 1982. *Cat on the Mat*. London: Oxford Press.

Williams, S. 1990. *I Went Walking*. New York: Harcourt Brace & Company.

———. 1998. *Let's Go Visiting*. New York: Harcourt Brace & Company.

Wise-Brown, M. I975. *Goodnight Moon*. New York: Harper Collins Publishers.

Young, R. 1997. *Who Says Moo?* New York: Puffin Books: Penguin Books Ltd.

Ziefert, H. 2000. *Grandma's Are for Giving Tickles*. New York: Puffin Books, The Penguin Group.

———. 2000. *Grandpa's Are for Finding Worms*. New York: Puffin Books, The Penguin Group.

Zolotow, C. 1958. *Do You Know What I'll Do?* New York: Harper Collins Publishers.

POETRY, RHYMING BOOKS, AND SONGS

Poetry Books

Chorao, K. 1984. *The Baby's Bedtime Book.* New York: Penguin Publishers.
de Paola, T. 1985. *Tomie de Paola's Mother Goose.* New York: Putnam.
Lansky, B. 1996. *Poetry Party.* New York: Simon & Schuster.
Lee, D. 1991. *The Ice Cream Store.* Toronto: Harper Collins.
———. 1987. *Alligator Pie.* Toronto: Macmillan of Canada.
Lotteridge, C. 1994. *Mother Goose: A Canadian Sampler.* Toronto: A Ground-
    wood Book: Douglas & McIntyre.
Opie, I. 1996. *My Very First Mother Goose.* Cambridge, MA: Candlewick.
Prelutsky, J. 1984. *The New Kid on the Block.* New York: Scholastic.
Silverstein, S. 1974. *Where the Sidewalk Ends.* New York: Harper Collins
    Publishers.
———. 1996. *Falling Up.* New York: Harper Collins Publishers.
Wildsmith, B. 1964. *Mother Goose.* London: Oxford Press.

Rhyming Predictable Pattern Books

Alborough, J. 2000. *Duck in the Truck.* New York: Harper Collins.
Blackstone, S. 1998. *Bear on a Bike.* New York: Barefoot Books.
Bogart, J. 1994. *Gifts.* Richmond Hill: Scholastic Canada.
Boynton, S. 2000. *Hippos Go Berserk!* New York: Little Simon, an Imprint of
    Simon & Schuster Children's Publishing Division.
Cherry, L. 1999. *Who's Sick Today?* New York: Scholastic.
Christelow, E. 1989. *Five Little Monkeys Jumping on the Bed.* New York:
    Scholastic.
Cutler, E. 1985. *If I Were a Cat I Would Sit in a Tree.* Montreal, Quebec,
    Canada: A Tundra Book.
de Paola, T. 1984. *Mice Squeak: We Speak.* New York: G. P. Putnam's Sons,
    The Putnam & Grosset Group.
Duke, K. 1985. *Seven Froggies Went to School.* New York: E. P. Dutton.
Facklam, M. 1999. *Bugs for Lunch.* Waterdown, MA: Charlesbridge Publishing.
Fitch, S. 1992. *There Were Monkeys in My Kitchen!* Toronto: Doubleday
    Canada Ltd.
Hutchins, P. 1978. *The Wind Blew.* New York: Viking Penguin.
Jorgensen, G. 1988. *Crocodile Beat.* New York: Scholastic.
Keats, E. 1975. *Over in the Meadow.* New York: Scholastic Book Services.
Krauss, R. 1948. *Bears.* New York: Scholastic Book Services.
Langstaff, J. 1984. *Oh, A Hunting We Will Go.* New York: Atheneum.
Lindberg, R. 1995. *The Midnight Farm.* New York: Puffin Pied Piper Books,
    The Penguin Group.
———. 1990. *The Day the Goose Got Loose.* New York: Penguin.
Lyon, G. 1994. *Together.* New York: Orchard Books.
Magnuson, K. 1998. *A Cake All for Me!* New York: Scholastic.
Miranda, M. 1997. *To Market, to Market.* New York: Harcourt Brace &
    Company.
Pienkowski, J. 1999. *Good Night.* Cambridge, MA: Candelwick Press.
Reid, B. 1992. *Two By Two.* Richmond Hill, Ontario: North Winds Press.
Sendak, M. 1962. *Chicken Soup with Rice.* New York: Scholastic Book Services.

Sutton, E. 1983. *My Cat Likes to Hide in Boxes.* New York: Puffin Books.

Walton, R. 2000. *One More Bunny.* New York: Lothrop, Lee & Shepard Books

Ward, P. 1997. *I Promise I'll Find You.* Willowdale, Ontario: Firefly Books Ltd.

Wood, A. 1982. *Quick as a Cricket.* New York: Child's Play International.

Young, R. 1997. *Who Says Moo?* New York: Puffin Books, Penguin Group, Penguin Books, USA.

Zolotow, C. 1983. *Some Things Go Together.* New York: Harper & Row.

Songs

Adams, P. 1974. *This Old Man.* New York: Child's Play International.

Barrett, C. 1984. *Mother Goose Song Book.* London: Heinemann.

Berry, H. 1994. *Old McDonald Had a Farm.* New York: Scholastic.

Dann, P. 1998. *Eensy Weensy Spider.* New York: Barron's Educational Series.

Kennedy, J. 1987. *The Teddy Bears' Picnic.* New York: Peter Bedrick Books.

Kovalski, M. 1987. *The Wheels on the Bus.* Toronto: Kids Can Press.

La Prise, L., C. Macak & T. Baker. 1997. *The Hokey Pokey.* New York: Scholastic.

Westcott, N. 1990. *There's a Hole in My Bucket.* New York: Scholastic.

SEQUENTIAL PREDICTABLE PATTERN BOOKS

Adams, P. 1979. *There Were Ten in a Bed.* New York: Child's Play International.

Allbright, V. 1985. *Ten Go Hopping.* Boston: Faber & Faber.

Baker, K. 1991. *Hide and Snake.* New York: Harcourt Brace Javanovich.

Barton, B. 1979. *Buzz Buzz Buzz.* New York: Macmillan Publishing Co.

Baum, A. & J. Baum. 1973. *One Bright Monday Morning.* New York: Pinwheel Books, Knopf Pantheon.

Brown, R. 1985. *The Big Sneeze.* Toronto: Stoddart Publishing: A Division of General Publishing.

Carle, E. 1993. *Today Is Monday.* New York: The Putnam & Grosset Group.

Christelow, E. 1989. *Five Little Monkeys Jumping on the Bed.* New York: Scholastic.

Crews, D. 1978. *Freight Train.* New York: Scholastic.

———. 1982. *Harbor.* New York: Greenwillow Books, William Morrow & Company.

———. 1989. *Flying.* New York: Greenwillow Books, William Morrow & Company.

———. 1995. *Sail Away.* Greenwillow Books, William Morrow & Company.

Ehlert, L. 1991. *Red Leaf, Yellow Leaf.* Orlando, Florida: Harcourt Brace & Company.

———. 1995. *Snowballs.* Orlando, Florida: Harcourt Brace & Company.

Ginsburg, M. 1972. *The Chick and the Duckling.* New York: Aladdin Books, Macmillan.

———. 1980. *Good Morning Chick.* New York: Scholastic.

Ginsburg, N. 1985. *Across the Stream.* New York: Puffin Books, Penguin Books.

Hill, E. 1986. *Spot Goes to the Circus*. New York: Puffin Books, Penguin
Books USA Inc.
———. 1990. *Spot Goes to the Farm*. New York: Puffin Books.
———. 1992. *Spot Goes to the Party*. New York: Putnam's Sons.
———. 1996. *Spot Visits His Grandparents*. New York: Puffin Books, Penguin
Books for Young Readers.
———. 1997. *Spot Bakes a Cake*. New York: Puffin Books, Penguin Books
USA.
———. 1999. *Spot Can Count*. New York: G. P. Putnam's Sons.
Krauss, R. 1945. *The Carrot Seed*. New York: Scholastic.
Magnuson, K. 1998. *A Cake All for Me!* New York: Scholastic.
McPhail, D. 1987. *First Flight*. New York: Little Brown & Company.
Newlin-Chase, E. 1993. *Water*. Richmond Hill, Ontario: North Winds Press:
Scholastic Canada.
Rice, E. 1983. *Goodnight, Goodnight*. New York: Penguin Books.
Rose, G. 1975. *Trouble in the Ark*. London: The Bodley Head.
Taback, S. 1999. *Joseph Had a Little Overcoat*. New York: Viking: Penguin
Putnam Books.
Wildsmith, B. 1982. *Cat on the Mat*. London: Oxford Press.
———. 1983. *All Fall Down*. London: Oxford Press.

CUMULATIVE PREDICTABLE PATTERN BOOKS

Allbright, V. 1985. *Ten Go Hopping*. London: Faber and Faber.
Aylesworth, J. 1989. *Mr. McGill Goes to Town*. New York: Henry Holt and
Company.
Fox, M. 1992. *Shoes from Grandpa*. New York: Orchard Books.
Jackson, A. 1997. *I Know an Old Lady Who Swallowed a Pie*. New York: Dut-
ton Children's Books, a Division of Penguin Books.
Lobel, A. 1984. *The Rose in My Garden*. New York: Greenwillow Books:
William Morrow & Company.
Peppe, R. 1985. *The House That Jack Built*. New York: Delacorte.
Robart, R. 1986. *The Cake That Mack Ate*. Toronto: Kids Can Press.
Wildsmith, B. 1983. *All Fall Down*. London: Oxford University Press.
Wood, A. 1984. *The Napping House*. Orlando: Harcourt Brace & Co.
Wyllie, S. & M. Roffey. 1985. *There Was an Old Woman*. New York: Harper
& Row.

REFRAIN BOOKS

Easy-Read Refrain Books

Carle, E. 1973. *Have You Seen My Cat?* New York: Putnam & Grosset Book
Group.
———. 1977. *The Grouchy Ladybug*. New York: Harper Collins.
———. 1984. *The Very Busy Spider*. New York: Scholastic.
———. 1987. *The Very Hungry Caterpillar*. New York: Philomel Books.

————. 1990. *The Very Quiet Cricket*. New York: Putnam & Grosset Book Group.

————. 1993. *Today Is Monday*. New York: Putnam & Grosset Group.

————. 1995. *The Very Lonely Firefly*. New York: Philomel Books.

————. 1997. *From Head to Toe*. New York: Scholastic.

————. 1998. *Hello, Red Fox*. New York: Simon & Schuster Books for Young Readers.

————. 1999. *Rooster's Off to See the World*. New York: Aladdin Paperbacks, an Imprint of Simon & Schuster.

————. 1999. *The Very Clumsy Click Beetle*. New York: Philomel Books.

Flack, M. 1971. *Ask Mr. Bear*. New York: Aladdin Paperbacks.

Fox, M. 1990. *Shoes From Grandpa*. New York: Orchard Books, A Division of Franklin Watts.

————. 1992. *Hattie and the Fox*. New York: Aladdin Books, Macmillan Publishing Company.

Gag, W. 1988. *Millions of Cats*. New York: Sandcastle books, A Division of The Putnam & Grosset Group.

Goss, J. & J. Harste. 1981. *It Didn't Frighten Me*. New York: School Book Fairs.

Hutchins, P. 1986. *The Doorbell Rang*. New York: Greenwillow.

Langstaff, J. 1984. *Oh, A Hunting We Will Go*. New York: Atheneum.

Mathews, J. & F. Robinson. 1999. *Nathaniel Willy, Scared Silly*. New York: Aladdin Paperbacks, an Imprint of Simon & Schuster.

Mayer, M. 1975. *Just for You*. Racine, Wisconsin: Western Publishing Company.

————. 1977. *Just Me and My Dad*. Racine, Wisconsin: Western Publishing Company.

————. 1983. *The New Baby*. Racine, Wisconsin: Western Publishing Company.

Munsch, R. 1985. *Mortimer*. Willowdale, Ontario: Annick Press.

————. 1989. *Fifty Below Zero*. Willowdale, Ontario: Annick Press.

————. 1992. *Purple, Green and Yellow*. Willowdale, Ontario: Annick Press.

————. 1998. *I Have to Go*. Willowdale, Ontario: Annick Press.

————. 2000. *Mmm, Cookies!* Markham, Ontario: Scholastic Canada.

Murphy, J. 1982. *Peace at Last*. New York: Dial Books for Young Readers, A Division of Penguin Books.

Newlin-Chase, E. 1984. *The New Baby Calf*. Richmond Hill, Ontario: Scholastic-TAB Publications Ltd.

Nodset, J. 1963. *Who Took the Farmer's Hat?* New York: Scholastic Books.

Slobodkina, E. 1968. *Caps for Sale*. New York: Scholastic.

Tafuri, N. 1998. *1 Love You, Little One*. New York: Scholastic.

Ward, H. 1997. *I Promise I'll Find You*. New York: Firefly Books USA.

Watson, J. 1988. *Grandpa's Slippers*. New York: Scholastic.

Weiss, N. 1990. *Where Does the Brown Bear Go?* New York: Puffin Books, The Penguin Group.

Wise-Brown, M. 1972. *The Runaway Bunny*. New York: Harper & Row, Publishers.

Wyllie, S. & Roffey, M. 1985. *There Was an Old Woman*. New York: Harper & Row, Publishers.

Traditional Refrain Books

Asbjornsen, P. "The Three Billy Goats Gruff. " In *Favorite Nursery Tales*, ed.
    T. de Paola, 42–45. New York: Putnam's Sons.
de Paola, T. 1986. *Favorite Nursery Tales.* New York: G. P. Putnam's Sons,
    The Putnam & Grosset Group.
Galdone, P. 1972. *The Three Bears.* New York: Seabury.
Hutchinson, V. 1976. *Henny Penny.* Boston: Little Brown.
Marshall, J. 1989. *Goldilocks and the Three Bears.* New York: Dial.
Reinl, E. 1983. *The Three Little Pigs.* Natic Mass: Picture Book Studio.
Zemach, M. 1983. *The Little Red Hen.* New York: Farrar, Straus and Giroux.

COMPLEX PICTURE BOOKS

Bourgeois, P. 1986. *Franklin in the Dark.* Toronto: Kids Can Press.
———. 1987. *Big Sarah's Little Boots.* Toronto: Kids Can Press.
———. 1989. *Hurry Up Franklin.* Toronto: Kids Can Press.
———. 1991. *Franklin Fibs.* Toronto: Kids Can Press.
———. 1992. *Franklin Is Lost.* Toronto: Kids Can Press.
———. 1993. *Franklin Is Bossy.* Toronto: Kids Can Press.
———. 1994. *Franklin Is Messy.* Toronto: Kids Can Press.
———. 1995. *Franklin and the Tooth Fairy.* Toronto: Kids Can Press.
———. 1995. *Franklin Goes to School.* Toronto: Kids Can Press.
———. 1995. *Franklin Plays the Game.* Toronto: Kids Can Press.
———. 1995. *Franklin Wants a Pet.* Toronto: Kids Can Press.
———. 1995. *Franklin's Blanket.* Toronto: Kids Can Press.
———. 1996. *Franklin Has a Sleep Over.* Toronto: Kids Can Press.
———. 1996. *Franklin's Bad Day.* Toronto: Kids Can Press.
———. 1996. *Franklin's School Play.* Toronto: Kids Can Press.
———. 1997. *Finders Keepers for Franklin.* Toronto: Kids Can Press.
———. 1997. *Franklin's New Friend.* Toronto: Kids Can Press.
———. 1997. *Franklin Rides a Bike.* Toronto: Kids Can Press.
———. 1998. *Franklin and the Thunder Storm.* Toronto: Kids Can Press.
———. 1998. *Franklin's Christmas Gift.* Toronto: Kids Can Press.
———. 1999. *Franklin and the Baby.* Toronto: Kids Can Press.
———. 1999. *Franklin Says Sorry.* Toronto: Kids Can Press.
———. 1999. *Franklin's Neighborhood.* Toronto: Kids Can Press.
———. 2000. *Franklin Goes to the Hospital.* Toronto: Kids Can Press.
Brett, J. 1985. *Annie and the Wild Animals.* Boston: Houghton Mifflin.
———. 1989. *The Mitten.* Boston: Houghton Mifflin.
———. 1997. *The Hat.* New York: G. P. Putnam's Sons.
Carle, E. 1999. *Rooster's off to See the World.* New York: Aladdin Paper Backs,
    an Imprint of Simon Schuster.
Fitch, S. 1994. *There Were Monkeys in My Kitchen.* Toronto: Doubleday,
    Canada.
Fox, M. 1988. *Koala Lou.* New York: Harcourt Brace Jovanovich.
George, K. 1995. *Incy-Wincy Spider.* Mississauga, Ontario, Canada. Fenn
    Publishing Co.

Grambling, L. 1995. *Can I Have a Stegosaurus, Mom? Can I Please!?* New York: Bridgewater Books.

Gray, N. 1995. *Running Away from Home.* New York: Random House.

Kellogg, S. 1986. *Best Friends.* New York: Dial Books.

Laminack, L. 1998. *Trevor's Wiggly-Wobbly Tooth.* Atlanta, Georgia: Peachtree Publishers.

Lobel, A. 1970. *Frog and Toad Are Friends.* New York: Harper & Row, Publishers.

———. 1972. *Frog and Toad Together.* New York: Scholastic Book Services.

Mathews, J. & F. Robinson. 1994. *Nathaniel Willy, Scared Silly.* New York: Aladdin Paperbacks, an Imprint of Simon & Schuster.

Mayer, M. 1980. *What Do You Do with a Kangaroo?* New York: Scholastic, Inc.

Morgan, A. 1985. *Sadie and the Snowman.* Toronto: Kids Can Press.

Munsch, R. 1979. *The Dark.* Toronto: Annick Press Ltd.

———. 1982. *Mud Puddle.* Toronto: Annick Press Ltd.

———. 1982. *Murmel, Murmel, Murmel.* Toronto: Annick Press Ltd.

———. 1983. *Angela's Airplane.* Toronto: Annick Press Ltd.

———. 1985. *Thomas' Snowsuit.* Toronto: Annick Press Ltd.

———. 1986. *The Boy in the Drawer.* Toronto: Annick Press Ltd.

———. 1989. *50 Below Zero.* Toronto: Annick Press Ltd.

———. 1989. *Pigs.* Toronto: Annick Press Ltd.

———. 1990. *Good Families Don't.* Toronto: Annick Press Ltd.

———. 1990. *Something Good.* Toronto: Annick Press Ltd.

———. 1991. *Show and Tell.* Toronto: Annick Press Ltd.

———. 1991. *The Fire Station.* Toronto: Annick Press Ltd.

———. 1995. *David's Father.* Toronto: Annick Press Ltd.

———. 1995. *Mortimer.* Toronto: Annick Press Ltd.

———. 1995. *The Dark.* Toronto: Annick Press Ltd.

———. 1995. *Wait and See.* Toronto: Annick Press Ltd.

———. 1995. *Where Is Gah-Ning?* Toronto: Annick Press Ltd.

———. 1996. *A Promise Is a Promise.* Toronto Annick Press Ltd.

———. 1996. *Purple, Green and Yellow.* Toronto: Annick Press Ltd.

———. 1996. *Stephanie's Pony Tail.* Toronto: Annick Press Ltd.

———. 1997. *Alligator Baby.* Toronto: Annick Press Ltd.

———. 1998. *Andrew's Loose Tooth.* Toronto: Scholastic Canada Ltd.

———. 1998. *Get Out of Bed.* Toronto: Scholastic Canada Ltd.

———. 1998. *I Have to Go!* Toronto: Annick Press Ltd.

———. 1999. *The Paper Bag Princess.* Toronto: Annick Press Ltd.

———. 1999. *We Share Everything.* Toronto: Scholastic Canada Ltd.

———. 2000. *Mmmm, Cookies.* Toronto: Scholastic Canada Ltd.

Sendak, M. 1963. *Where the Wild Things Are.* New York: Scholastic Book Services.

Staunton, T. 1986. *Simon's Surprise.* Toronto: Kids Can Press.

Stinson, K. 1988. *Teddy Rabbit.* Toronto: Kids Can Press.

Viorst, J. 1987. *Alexander and the Terrible, Horrible, No Good, Very Bad Day.* New York: Aladdin, an Imprint of Simon & Schuster.

———. 1995. *Alexander, Who's Not (Do You Hear Me? I Mean It!) Going to Move.* New York: Athenium Books for Young Readers, an Imprint of Simon & Schuster.

Waber, B. 1972. *Ira Sleeps Over*. Boston: Houghton Mifflin Co.

Wildsmith, B. 1993. *The Owl and the Woodpecker*. London: Oxford University Press.

Yolen, J. 1988. *Owl Moon*. New York: Philomel.

Issues Books

Browne, A. 1999. *Voices in the Park*. London: Transworld Publishers Ltd.

Bogart, J., L. Fernandez & R. Jacobson. *Jeremiah Learns to Read*. Markham, Ontario: Scholastic.

Brown, R. 1990. *The World That Jack Built*. Toronto: Stoddart.

Bunting, E. 1991. *Fly Away Home*. New York: Clarion Books, a Houghton Mifflin Company Imprint.

———. 1994. *Sunshine Home*. New York: Houghton Mifflin Company.

Cooney, B. 1994. *Only Opal, the Diary of a Young Girl*. New York: Putnam & Grosset Group.

Dillon, L. & D. Dillon, 1998. *To Everything There Is a Season*. New York: The Blue Sky Press, An Imprint of Scholastic.

Duggan, B. 1992. *Loop the Loop*. New York: Greenwillow Books.

Fox, M. 1989. *Night Noises*. New York: Harcourt Brace & Company.

Frasier, D. 1991. *On the Day You Were Born*. New York: Scholastic.

Howe, J. 1999. *Horace and Morris But Mostly Delores*. New York: Scholastic.

Jukes, M. 1984. *Like Jake and Me*. New York: Dragonfly Books, Alfred Knopf.

King-Mitchell, M. 1993. *Uncle Jed's Barbershop*. New York: Scholastic.

Lorbiecki, M. 1998. *Sister Anne's Hands*. New York: Dial Books, a Member of Penguin Putnam.

Lyon, E. 1993. *Come a Tide*. New York: Orchard Books.

MacLachlan, P. 1994. *All the Places to Love*. New York: Harper Collins.

———. 1998. *What You Know First*. New York: Joanna Cotler Books, Harper Trophy.

Manson, A. 1995. *Just Like New*. Toronto: Douglas & McIntyre.

McGovern, A. 1997. *The Lady in the Box*. New York: Turtle Books.

McGugan, J. 1994. *Josepha, a Prairie Boys Story*. Red Deer, Alberta: Northern Lights Books for Children.

Rylant, C. 1997. *Cat Heaven*. New York: The Blue Sky Press, An Imprint of Scholastic.

Waddell, M. 1989. *Once There Were Giants*. Cambridge, MA: Candlewick Press.

Wild, M. & J. Vivas. 1990. *The Very Best of Friends*. Toronto: Kids Can Press.

Yolen, J. 1992. *Letting Swift River Go*. Boston: Little Brown and Company.

Zolotow, C. 1971. *A Father Like That*. New York: Harper and Row Publishers.

———. 1972. *William's Doll*. New York: Harper Trophy.

———. 1997. *Who Is Ben?* New York: Harper Collins Publishers.

SHARED READING: SELECTIONS SUITABLE FOR THE SHARED READING PROCESS

Adams, P. 1979. *There Were Ten in a Bed*. New York: Child's Play International.

Alborough, J. 2000. *Duck in the Truck*. New York: Harper Collins.

Allbright, V. 1985. *Ten Go Hopping.* London: Faber and Faber.

Asch, F. 1985. *I Can Roar.* Toronto: Kids Can Press.

———. 1997. *I Can Blink.* Toronto: Kids Can Press.

Baum, A. and J. Baum. 1973. *One Bright Monday Morning.* New York: Pinwheel Books, Knopf Pantheon.

Berry, H. 1994. *Old McDonald Had a Farm.* New York: Scholastic.

Brown, R. 1985. *The Big Sneeze.* Toronto: Stoddart Publishing: A Division of General Publishing.

Burningham, J. 1984. *Would You Rather . . .* London: Picture Lions.

Campbell, R. 1985. *Dear Zoo.* New York: Viking Penguin.

Carle, E. 1997. *From Head to Toe.* New York: Scholastic.

———. 2000. *Does a Kangaroo Have a Mother, Too?* New York: Harper Collins.

Chang, C. 1996. *Are You My Baby?* New York: Intervisual Books and Random House.

Christelow, E. 1989. *Five Little Monkeys Jumping on the Bed.* New York: Scholastic.

Dann, P. 1998. *Eensy Weensy Spider.* New York: Barron's Educational Series, Inc.

de Paola, T. 1980. *If He's My Brother.* Englewood Cliffs, NJ: Prentice-Hall, Inc.

———. 1984. *Mice Squeak: We Speak.* New York: G. P. Putnam's Sons, The Putnam & Grosset Group.

Ginsburg, M. 1972. *The Chick and the Duckling.* New York: Aladdin Books, Macmillan Publishing.

Hutchins, P. 1972. *Good Night Owl!* New York: Macmillan Publishing Co.

Kovalski, M. 1987. *The Wheels on the Bus.* Toronto: Kids Can Press.

Krauss, R. 1948. *Bears.* New York: Scholastic Book Services.

———. 2000. *Whose Mouse Are You?* New York: Simon & Schuster.

Lacome, J. 1992. *Noisy Noises on the Farm.* London: Walker Books.

Langstaff, J. 1984. *Oh, A Hunting We Will Go.* New York: Atheneum.

London, J. 1999. *Wiggle Waggle.* San Diego: Harcourt Brace & Company.

———. 2000. *Snuggle Wuggle.* San Diego: Harcourt Brace & Company.

Lyon, G. 1994. *Together.* New York: Orchard Books.

Martin, B. Jr. 1991. *Polar Bear, Polar Bear, What Do You Hear?* New York: Henry Holt & Company.

———. 1992. *Brown Bear, Brown Bear, What Do You See?* New York: Henry Holt & Company.

Pandell, K. 1994. *I Love You, Sun. I Love You, Moon.* New York: Putnam's Sons.

Pienkowski, J. 1999. *Good Night.* Cambridge, MA: Candelwick Press.

Rose, G. 1975. *Trouble in the Ark.* London: The Bodley Head.

Tafuri, N. 1997. *What the Sun Sees: What the Moon Sees.* New York: Scholastic.

Watanabe, S. 1982. *I Can Ride It!* New York: Philomel Books: Putnam Publishing.

———. 1984. *How Do I Put It On?* New York: Penguin Books.

Wildsmith, B. 1982. *Cat on the Mat.* London: Oxford Press.

———. 1983. *All Fall Down.* London: Oxford Press.

Williams, S. 1990. *I Went Walking.* New York: Harcourt Brace & Company.

———. 1998. *Let's Go Visiting.* New York: Harcourt Brace & Company.

Wood, A. 1982. *Quick as a Cricket.* New York: Child's Play International.

Young, R. 1997. *Who Says Moo?* New York: Puffin Books: Penguin Books Ltd.
Zolotow, C. 1958. *Do You Know What I'll Do?* New York: Harper Collins
    Publishers.
———. 1983. *Some Things Go Together*. New York: Harper & Row.

WORD BOOKS: BOOKS TO EMPHASIZE WORD STUDY

Highlighted Words: Selections That Highlight Words

Carle, E. 2000. *Does a Kangaroo Have a Mother, Too?* New York: Harper
    Collins.
Gugler, L. 1997. *Muddle Cuddle*. Toronto: Annick Press.
Jackson, A. 1997. *I Know an Old lady Who Swallowed a Pie*. New York: Dutton.
Martin, B. Jr. 1999. *A Beasty Story*. New York: Harcourt Brace & Company.
Miranda, M. 1997. *To Market, to Market*. New York: Harcourt Brace &
    Company.
Wyllie, S. & M. Roffey. 1985. *There Was an Old Woman*. New York: Harper
    & Row.

Books That Emphasize Words for Parts of the Body

Adams, P. 1974. *This Old Man*. New York: Child's Play International.
La Prise, L., C. Macak & T. Baker. 1997. *The Hokey Pokey*. New York:
    Scholastic.

Color Words: Books That Highlight Color Words

Carle, E. 1987. *The Very Hungry Caterpillar*. New York: Philomel Books.
Carle, E. 1998. *Hello Red Fox*. New York: Simon & Schuster Books for Young
    Children.
Crews, D. 1978. *Freight Train*. New York: Scholastic.
Ehlert, L. 1990. *Color Zoo*. New York: Lippincott.
Gerstein, M. 1983. *Follow Me*. New York: William Morrow and Company.
Jona, A. 1989. *Color Dance*. New York: Greenwillow.
Martin, B. Jr. 1991. *Brown Bear, Brown Bear, What Do You See?* New York:
    Henry Holt & Company.
———. 1999. *A Beasty Story*. New York: Harcourt Brace & Company.
Stinson, K. 1982. *Red Is Best*. Toronto: Annick Press Ltd.
Williams, S. 1990. *I Went Walking*. New York: Harcourt Brace & Company.
———. 1998. *Let's Go Visiting*. New York: Harcourt Brace & Company.

Concept Word Books: Books That Employ Terms (over, under, through, beside, etc.)

Baker, K. 1991. *Hide and Snake*. New York: Harcourt Brace Jovanovich.
Crews, D. 1995. *Sail Away*. New York: Greenwillow Books, William Morrow
    & Company.
Duke, K. 1984. *Guinea Pigs Far and Near*. New York: E. P. Dutton.
Ginsberg, M. 1985. *Across the Stream*. New York: Viking Penguin.
Hill, E. 1980. *Where's Spot*. New York: Puffin Books.

Hoban, T. 1973. *Over, Under and Through and Other Spatial Concepts.* New York: Macmillan.
Hutchins, P. 1968. *Rosie's Walk.* New York: Macmillan.

Descriptive Words: Books That Have Descriptive Language

Campbell, R. 1982. *Dear Zoo.* New York: Viking, Penguin.
Gugler, L. 1997. *Muddle Cuddle.* Toronto: Annick Press.
London, J. 1997. *Puddles.* Puffin Books, The Penguin Group.
Wildsmith, B. 1989. *What a Tale.* London: Oxford Press.
Wood, A. 1982. *Quick as a Cricket.* New York: Child's Play International.
Wise-Brown, M. 1977. *The Important Book.* New York: Harper Collins.

Action Words: Books That Employ Action Words

Asch, F. 1997. *I Can Blink.* Toronto: Kids Can Press.
Kovalski, M. 1987. *The Wheels on the Bus.* Toronto: Kids Can Press.
de Paola, T. 1984. *Mice Squeak, We Speak.* New York: G. P. Putnam's Sons, The Putnam & Grosset Group.
Hutchins, P. 1976. *Good-Night, Owl.* New York: Macmillan Publishing Co.
London, J. 1999. *Wiggle Waggle.* New York: Harcourt Brace & Company.
————. 2000. *Snuggle Wuggle.* New York: Harcourt Brace & Company.
Rose, G. 1985. *Trouble in the Ark.* London: Bodley Head.
Wildsmith, B. 1982. *Cat on the Mat.* London: Oxford Press.
Wood, A. 1982. *Quick as a Cricket.* New York: Child's Play International.

Animal Words: Books That Emphasize Animal Names

1. Books with General Animal Words

Allbright, V. 1985. *Ten Go Hopping.* Boston: Faber & Faber.
de Paola, T. 1984. *Mice Squeak, We Speak.* New York: G. P. Putnam's Sons, The Putnam & Grosset Group.
Hutchins, P. 1976. *Good-Night, Owl.* New York: Macmillan Publishing Co.
Kitchen, B. 1984. *Animal Alphabet.* New York: Dial.
Kraus, R. 2000. *Whose Mouse Are You?* New York: Simon & Schuster.
London, J. 1999. *Wiggle Waggle.* New York: Harcourt Brace & Company.
London, J. 2000. *Snuggle Wuggle.* New York: Harcourt Brace & Company.
Rose, G. 1985. *Trouble in the Ark.* London: Bodley Head.
Wildsmith, B. 1982. *Cat on the Mat.* London: Oxford Press.
Wood, A. 1982. *Quick as a Cricket.* New York: Child's Play International.

2. Farm Animal Theme

Barton, B. 1979. *Buzz Buzz Buzz.* New York: Macmillan Publishing Co.
Brown, R. 1985. *The Big Sneeze.* Toronto: Stoddart Publishing: A Division of General Publishing.
Chang, C. 1996. *Are You My Baby?* New York: Intervisual Books and Random House.
Flack, M. 1960. *Ask Mr. Bear.* New York: Aladdin.
Fox, M. 1992. *Hattie and the Fox.* New York: Aladdin Books, Macmillan Publishing Company.

Ginsburg, M. 1972. *The Chick and the Duckling.* New York: Aladdin Books, Macmillan.

———. 1980. *Good Morning Chick.* New York: Scholastic Inc.

———. 1985. *Across the Stream.* New York: Puffin Books, Penguin Books.

Hill, E. 1990. *Spot Goes to the Farm.* New York: Puffin.

Hill, E. 1996. *Spot Visits His Grandparents.* New York: Puffin Books, Penguin Books for Young Readers.

Lindberg, R. 1995. *The Midnight Farm.* New York: Puffin Pied Piper Books, The Penguin Group.

Martin, B. Jr. 1992. *Brown Bear, Brown Bear, What Do You See?* New York: Henry Holt & Company.

Williams, S. 1989. *I Went Walking.* New York: Harcourt Brace & Company.

Wood, A. 1984. *The Napping House.* Orlando Florida: Harcourt Brace & Company.

Wyllie, S. & M. Roffey. 1985. *There Was an Old Woman.* New York: Harper & Row.

3. Zoo Animals

Asch, F. 1985. *I Can Roar.* Toronto: Kids Can Press.

Carle, E. 2000. *Does a Kangaroo Have a Mother, Too?* New York: Harper Collins.

Christelow, E. 1989. *Five Little Monkeys Jumping on the Bed.* New York: Scholastic.

Hill, E. 1986. *Spot Goes to the Circus.* New York: Puffin Books, Penguin Books USA.

Martin, B. Jr. 1991. *Polar Bear, Polar Bear, What Do You Hear?* Henry Holt and Company.

4. Insects: Books That Repeat Names of Insects

Baker, J. 1982. *One Hungry Spider.* London: Andre Deutsch Ltd.

Carle, E. 1977. *The Grouchy Ladybug.* New York: Harper Collins.

———. 1985. *The Very Busy Spider.* New York: Scholastic.

———. 1987. *The Very Hungry Caterpillar.* New York: Philomel Books.

———. 1990. *The Very Quiet Cricket.* New York: Putnam & Grosset Book Group.

———. 1995. *The Very Lonely Firefly.* New York: Philomel Books.

———. 1999. *The Very Clumsy Click Beetle.* New York: Philomel Books.

Facklam, M. 1996. *Creepy Crawly Caterpillars.* Boston: Little Brown.

———. 1999. *Bugs for Lunch.* Waterdown, MA: Charlesbridge Publishing.

ALPHABET BOOKS

Bayer, J. 1984. *A, My Name Is Alice.* New York: Dial.

Ehlert, L. 1989. *Eating the Alphabet.* New York: Harcourt Brace Jovanovich Publishers.

Kitchen, B. 1984. *Animal Alphabet.* New York: Dial.

Lobel, A. 1981. *On Market Street.* New York: Scholastic.

Martin, B. Jr. & J. Archambault, 1989. *Chicka Chika Boom Boom.* New York: Simon & Schuster.
Pilcher, S. 1982. *Elfabit.* Burlington, Ontario, Canada: Hayes Publishing.
Pallotta, J. 1989. *The Icky Bug Alphabet Book.* Waterdown, MA: Charlesbridge.

INFORMATIONAL MATERIAL

1. Nonfiction Informational Books

Arnosky, J. 1993. *Every Autumn Comes the Bear.* New York: Putnam & Grosset Group.
———. 1995. *I See Animals Hiding.* New York: Scholastic.
Barton, B. 1981. *Building a House.* New York: Greenwillow.
———. 1982. *Airport.* New York: Harper & Row.
———. 1987. *Machines at Work.* New York: Crowell.
———. 1988. *I Want to Be an Astronaut.* New York: Crowell.
———. 1989. *Bones, Bones, Dinosaur Bones.* New York: Harper Collins.
———. 1989. *Dinosaurs, Dinosaurs.* New York: Crowell.
Bingham, C. 1994. *The Big Book of Things That Go.* Toronto: Scholastic, TAB.
Bourgeois, P. 1987. *The Amazing Apple Book.* Toronto: Kids Can Press.
———. 1990. *The Amazing Dirt Book.* Toronto: Kids Can Press.
Burningham, J. 1985. *Opposites.* New York: Crown Books.
Cole, J. 1976. *A Chick Hatches.* New York: Morrow.
———. 1985. *The New Baby at Your House.* New York: Morrow.
Crews, D. 1980. *Truck.* New York: Greenwillow.
Facklam, M. 1996. *Creepy Crawly Caterpillars.* Boston: Little, Brown.
Fowler, A. 1990. *It's a Good Thing There Are Insects.* Chicago: Children's Press.
Gibbons, G. 1966. *Flying.* New York: Holiday House.
———. 1982. *Tool Book.* New York: Holiday House.
———. 1984. *Fire! Fire!* New York: Harper & Row.
———. 1987. *Dinosaurs.* New York: Holiday House.
———. 1989. *Monarch Butterfly.* New York: Holiday House.
———. 1993. *Spiders.* New York: Holiday House.
Godkin, C. 1995. *What About Ladybugs?* New York: Sierra.
Goudey, A. 1964. *Butterfly Time.* New York: Scribners.
Green, J. 1993. *Backyard Bear.* New York: Scholastic.
Heiligman, D. 1996. *From Caterpillar to Butterfly.* New York: Harper Collins.
Heller, R. 1985. *How to Hide a Butterfly and Other Insects.* New York: Grosset & Dunlap.
Jordon, H. 1960. *How a Seed Grows.* New York: Thomas Y. Crowell.
Micucci, C. 1995. *The Life and Times of the Honey-Bee.* New York: Ticknor.
Morris, J. 1995. *Bears, Bears, and More Bears.* New York: Barrons Educational Series.
Reid, B. 1991. *Zoe's Rainy Day.* Toronto: Harper Collins.
———. 1991. *Zoe's Snowy Day.* Toronto: Harper Collins.
———. 1991. *Zoe's Sunny Day.* Toronto: Harper Collins.
———. 1991. *Zoe's Windy Day.* Toronto: Harper Collins.
Rockwell, H. 1985. *The Emergency Room.* New York: Macmillan.

Schoenherr, J. 1991. *Bear*. New York: The Putnam & Grosset Group.
Watts, B. 1987. *Ladybug*. Morristown, New Jersey: Silver Burdett.
Ziegler, S. 1988. *A Visit to the Airport*. Chicago: Children's Press.

2. Informational Material in Fictional Books

Baker, J. 1982. *One Hungry Spider*. London: Andre Deutsch Ltd.
Briggs, R. 1985. *Building the Snowman*. Boston: Little, Brown.
Brinckloe, J. 1974. *The Spider Web*. New York: Doubleday.
———. 1985. *Fireflies!* New York: Aladdin.
Carle, E. 1969. *The Very Hungry Caterpillar*. New York: Philomel.
———. 1977. *The Grouchy Ladybug*. New York: Crowel.
———. 1990. *The Very Quiet Cricket*. New York: Philomel.
———. 1995. *The Very Lonely Firefly*. New York: Philomel.
———. 1999. *The Very Clumsy Click Beetle*. New York: Philomel.
Cherry, L. 1990. *The Great Kapok Tree*. San Diego, CA: Harcourt Brace
   Jovanovich.
Croft, R. 1975. *Winter Bear*. New York: Aladdin.
Ehlert, L. 1991. *Red Leaf, Yellow Leaf*. New York: Harcourt Brace & Company.
Fleming, D. 1997. *Time to Sleep*. New York: Scholastic.
Ginsberg, M. 1980. *Good Morning Chick*. New York: Scholastic.
Howe, J. 1985. *I Wish I Were a Butterfly* . San Diego, CA: Harcourt Brace
   Jovanovich.
Krauss, R. 1945. *The Carrot Seed*. New York: Harper & Row.
Lind, A. 1994. *Black Bear Cub*. New York: Scholastic.
McCloskey, R. 1976. *Blueberries for Sal*. New York: Scholastic.
McPhail, D. 1987. *First Flight*. New York: Little, Brown.
Ormerod, J. 1986. *Just Like Me*. New York: Lothrop, Lee & Shepard.
Pallotta, J. 1989. *The Icky Bug Alphabet Book*. Waterdown, MA:
   Charlesbridge.
Pomerantz, C. 1984. *Where's Bear?* New York: Greenwillow.
Windslow-Parker, N. 1987. *Bugs*. New York: Greenwillow.
Yolen, J. 1987. *Owl Moon*. New York: Philomel.

THEME STUDIES

Animal Themes

1. General Animal Theme Books

Allbright, V. 1985. *Ten Go Hopping*. Boston: Faber & Faber.
Asch, F. 1997. *I Can Blink*. Toronto: Kids Can Press.
Brett, J. 1985. *Annie and the Wild Animals*. Boston: Houghton Mifflin.
———. 1989. *The Mitten*. Boston: Houghton Mifflin.
———. 1997. *The Hat*. New York: Putnam's Sons.
de Paola, T. 1984. *Mice Squeak, We Speak*. New York: G. P. Putnam's Sons,
   The Putnam & Grosset Group.
Hutchins, P. 1976. *Good-Night, Owl*. New York: Macmillan Publishing Co.
Kitchen, B. 1984. *Animal Alphabet*. New York: Dial.
Kraus, R. 2000. *Whose Mouse Are You?* New York: Simon & Schuster.

London, J. 1999. *Wiggle Waggle*. New York: Harcourt Brace & Company.
——. 2000. *Snuggle Wuggle*. New York: Harcourt Brace & Company.
Nodset, J. 1963. *Who Took the Farmer's Hat*. New York: Scholastic Books.
Rose, G. 1985. *Trouble in the Ark*. London: Bodley Head.
Tafuri, N. 1998. *I Love You, Little One*. New York: Scholastic.
Wildsmith, B. 1982. *Cat on the Mat*. London: Oxford Press.
——. 1993. *The Owl and the Woodpecker*. London: Oxford Press.
Wood, A. 1982. *Quick as a Cricket*. New York: Child's Play International.
Yolen, J. 1987. *Owl Moon*. New York: Philomel.

2. Farm Animal Theme Books

Barton, B. 1979. *Buzz Buzz, Buzz*. New York: Macmillan Publishing Co.
Berry, H. 1994. *Old MacDonald Had a Farm*. New York: Scholastic.
Brown, R. 1985. *The Big Sneeze*. Toronto: Stoddart Publishing: A Division of General Publishing.
Chang, C. 1996. *Are You My Baby?* New York: Intervisual Books and Random House.
Cole, J. 1976. *A Chick Hatches*. New York: Morrow.
Flack, M. 1960. *Ask Mr. Bear*. New York: Aladdin.
Fox, M. 1992. *Hattie and the Fox*. New York: Aladdin Books, Macmillan Publishing Company.
Ginsburg, M. 1972. *The Chick and the Duckling*. New York: Aladdin Books, Macmillan.
Ginsberg, M. 1980. *Good Morning Chick*. New York: Scholastic.
Ginsberg, N. 1985. *Across the Stream*. New York: Puffin Books, Penguin Books.
Hill, E. 1990. *Spot Goes to the Farm*. New York: Puffin.
——. 1996. *Spot Visits His Grandparents*. New York: Puffin Books, Penguin Books for Young Readers.
Hutchins, P. 1968. *Rosie's Walk*. New York: Macmillan Co.
Lacome, J. 1992. *Noisy Noises on the Farm*. London: Walker Books.
Lindberg, R. 1995. *The Midnight Farm*. New York: Puffin Pied Piper Books, The Penguin Group.
Martin, B. Jr. 1992. *Brown Bear, Brown Bear, What Do You See?* New York: Henry Holt & Company.
Munsch, R. 1989. *Pigs*. Toronto: Annick Press.
Newlin-Chase, E. 1984. *The New Baby Calf*. Richmond Hill, Ontario: North Winds.
Williams, S. 1989. *I Went Walking*. New York: Harcourt Brace & Company.
Wood, A. 1984. *The Napping House*. Orlando, FL: Harcourt Brace & Company.
Wyllie, S. & M. Roffey. 1985. *There Was an Old Woman*. New York: Harper & Row.
Zemach, H. 1983. *The Little Red Hen*. New York: Farrar, Straus & Giroux.

3. Zoo Animal Theme

Asch, F. 1985. *I Can Roar*. Toronto: Kids Can Press.
Carle, E. 1973. *Have You Seen My Cat?* New York: Harper Collins.

———. 2000. *Does a Kangaroo Have a Mother, Too?* New York: Harper Collins.

Cherry, L. 1990. *The Great Kapok Tree.* San Diego, CA: Harcourt Brace Jovanovich.

Christelow, E. 1989. *Five Little Monkeys Jumping on the Bed.* New York: Scholastic.

Hill, E. 1986. *Spot Goes to the Circus.* New York: Puffin Books, Penguin Books USA.

Martin, B. Jr. 1991. *Polar Bear, Polar Bear, What Do You Hear?* Henry Holt and Company.

4. Bear Theme

Arnosky, J. 1993. *Every Autumn Comes the Bear.* New York: Putnam & Grosset Group.

———. 1995. *I See Animals Hiding.* New York: Scholastic.

Blackstone, S. 1998. *Bear on a Bike.* New York: Barefoot Books.

Croft, R. 1975. *Winter Bear.* New York: Aladdin.

Flack, M. 1971. *Ask Mr. Bear.* New York: Aladdin Paperbacks.

Fleming, D. 1997. *Time to Sleep.* New York: Scholastic.

Galdone, P. 1972. *The Three Bears.* New York: Seabury.

Green, J. 1993. *Backyard Bear.* New York: Scholastic.

Krauss, R. 1948. *Bears.* New York: Scholastic Book Services.

Lind, A. 1994. *Black Bear Cub.* New York: Scholastic.

Kennedy, J. 1987. *The Teddy Bears' Picnic.* New York: Peter Bedrick Books.

Marshall, J. 1989. *Goldilocks and the Three Bears.* New York: Dial.

Martin, B. Jr. 1991. *Polar Bear, Polar Bear, What Do You Hear?* Henry Holt and Company.

———. 1992. *Brown Bear, Brown Bear, What Do You See?* New York: Henry Holt & Company.

McCloskey, R. 1976. *Blueberries for Sal.* New York: Scholastic.

Morris, J. 1995. *Bears, Bears, and More Bears.* New York: Barrons Educational Series.

Pomerantz, C. 1984. *Where's Bear?* New York: Greenwillow.

Schoenherr, J. 1991. *Bear.* New York: The Putnam & Grosset Group.

Weiss, N. 1990. *Where Does the Brown Bear Go?* New York: Puffin Books, The Penguin Group.

Winter, P. 1976. *The Bear and the Fly.* New York: Scholastic.

5. Insect Theme

Baker, J. 1982. *One Hungry Spider.* London: Andre Deutsch Ltd.

Brinckloe, J. 1974. *The Spider Web.* New York: Doubleday.

———. 1985. *Fireflies!* New York: Aladdin.

Carle, E. 1977. *The Grouchy Ladybug.* New York: Harper Collins.

———. 1985. *The Very Busy Spider.* New York: Scholastic.

———. 1987. *The Very Hungry Caterpillar.* New York: Philomel Books.

———. 1990. *The Very Quiet Cricket.* New York: Putnam & Grosset Book Group.

———. 1995. *The Very Lonely Firefly.* New York: Philomel Books.

———. 1999. *The Very Clumsy Click Beetle.* New York: Philomel Books.

Dann, P. 1998. *Eency Weency Spider.* New York: Barron's Educational Series.

Facklam, M. 1996. *Creepy Crawly Caterpillars.* Boston: Little, Brown.

———. 1999. *Bugs for Lunch.* Watertown, MA: Charlesbridge Publishing.

Fowler, A. 1990. *It's a Good Thing There Are Insects.* Chicago: Children's Press.

George, K. 1995. *Incy-Wincy Spider.* Mississauga, Ontario: Fenn Publishing Co.

Gibbons, G. 1989. *Monarch Butterfly.* New York: Holiday House.

———. 1993. *Spiders.* New York: Holiday House.

Godkin, C. 1995. *What About Ladybugs?* New York: Sierra.

Goudey, A. 1964. *Butterfly Time.* New York: Scribners.

Heiligman, D. 1996. *From Caterpillar to Butterfly.* New York: Harper Collins.

Heller, R. 1985. *How to Hide a Butterfly and Other Insects.* New York: Grosset & Dunlop.

Howe, J. 1985. *I Wish I Were a Butterfly.* San Diego, CA: Harcourt Brace Jovanovich.

Micucci, C. 1995. *The Life and Times of the Honey-Bee.* New York: Ticknor.

Pallotta, J. 1989. *The Icky Bug Alphabet Book.* Waterdown, MA: Charlesbridge.

Watts, B. 1987. *Ladybug.* Morristown, New Jersey: Silver Burdett.

Windslow-Parker, N. 1987. *Bugs.* New York: Greenwillow.

Family

1. Members of Families

Alexander, M. 1971. *Nobody Asked Me If I Wanted a Baby Sister.* New York: Dial Press.

Bogart, J. 1994. *Gifts.* Richmond Hill, Ontario: Scholastic Canada.

Cole, J. 1985. *The New Baby at Your House.* New York: Morrow.

de Paola, T. 1981. *Now One Foot, Now the Other.* New York: G. P. Putnam's Sons.

Flack, M. 1960. *Ask Mr. Bear.* New York: Aladdin.

Gackenbach, D. 1989. *With Love from Gran.* New York: Clarion Books.

Galloway, P. 1980. *Good Times Bad Times.* Toronto: University of Toronto Press.

———. 1984. *When You Were Little and I Was Big.* Toronto: Annick Press.

Mayer, M. 1975. *Just for You.* Racine Wisconsin: Western Publishing Company.

———. 1977. *Just Me and My Dad.* Racine Wisconsin: Western Publishing Company.

———. 1983. *Just Grandma and Me.* Racine Wisconsin: Western Publishing Company.

———. 1985. *Just Grandpa and Me.* Racine Wisconsin: Western Publishing Company.

McPhail, D. 1984. *Fix It.* New York: Little, Brown.

McCully, E.M. 1988. *New Baby.* New York: Harper & Row.

Munsch, 1997. *Alligator Baby.* Toronto: Annick Press.

Murphy, J. 1986. *Five Minutes Peace.* London: Walker Books.

Quinlan, P. 1987. *My Dad Takes Care of Me.* Toronto: Annick Press.

Staunton, T. 1986. *Simon's Surprise.* Toronto: Kids Can Press.

Watson, J. 1989. *Grandpa's Slippers.* New York: Scholastic.

Wood, D. 2000. *What Dads Can't Do.* New York: Simon & Schuster.

Ziefert, H. 2000. *Grandmas Are for Giving Tickles.* New York: Puffin Books Ltd.

———. 2000. *Grandpas Are for Finding Worms.* New York: Puffin Books Ltd.

Zolotow, C. 1971. *A Father Like That.* New York: Harper & Row.

2. Bed Time Theme

Bourgeois, P. 1995. *Franklin's Blanket.* Toronto: Kids Can Press.

———. 1996. *Franklin Has a Sleep Over.* Toronto: Kids Can Press.

Hutchins, P. 1976. *Good Night Owl.* New York: Macmillan Publishing Co.

Mayer, M. 1986. *Just Me and My Baby Sitter.* Racine Wisconsin: Western Publishing Company.

Munsch, R. 1995. *Mortimer.* Toronto: Annick Press Ltd.

———. 1998. *Get Out of Bed.* Toronto: Annick Press Ltd.

Murphy, J. 1980. *Peace at Last.* New York: Dial Books for Young Readers, A Division of Penguin Books USA.

Pienkowski, J. 1999. *Good Night.* Cambridge MA: Candlewick Press.

Rice, E. 1980. *Good Night.* New York: Penguin Books.

Sendak, M. 1963. *Where the Wild Things Are.* New York: Scholastic, Inc.

Waber, B. 1972. *Ira Sleeps Over.* Boston: Houghton Mifflin.

Weiss, N. 1989. *Where Does Brown Bear Go?* New York: Puffin Books, The Penguin Books.

Wise-Brown, M. 1975. *Good Night Moon.* New York: Harper Collins Publishers.

Friends

Bourgeois, P. 1997. *Franklin's New Friend.* Toronto: Kids Can Press.

Carle, E. 1988. *Do You Want to Be My Friend?* New York: Putnam & Grosset Book Group.

Cohen, M. 1967. *Will I Have a Friend?* New York: Macmillan Publishing Co.

Heide, F. 1968. *That's What Are Friends For.* New York: Scholastic.

Kellogg, S. 1986. *Best Friends.* New York: Dial Books, A Division of E. P. Dutton.

Korth-Sander, I. 1986. *Will You Be My Friend?* London: North-South Books.

Lobel, A. 1972. *Frog and Toad Together.* New York: Scholastic Book Services.

———. 1970. *Frog and Toad Are Friends.* New York: Harper & Row, Publishers.

Mayer, M. 1977. *Frog Goes to Dinner.* New York: Dial books for Young Children, a Division of E. P. Dutton.

Color Theme

Carle, E. 1987. *The Very Hungry Caterpillar.* New York: Philomel Books.

———. 1998. *Hello Red Fox.* New York: Simon & Schuster Books for Young Children.

Crews, D. 1978. *Freight Train.* New York: Scholastic.

Gerstein, M. 1983. *Follow Me.* New York: William Morrow and Company.

Jona, A. 1989. *Color Dance.* New York: Greenwillow.
Martin, B. Jr. 1991. *Brown Bear, Brown Bear, What Do You See?* New York: Henry Holt & Company.
———. 1999. *A Beasty Story.* New York: Harcourt Brace & Company.
Stinson, K. 1982. *Red Is Best.* Toronto: Annick Press Ltd.
Williams, S. 1990. *I Went Walking.* New York: Harcourt Brace & Company.
———. 1998. *Let's Go Visiting.* New York: Harcourt Brace & Company.

Concept Word Theme (over, under, through, beside, etc.)

Baker, K. 1991. *Hide and Snake.* New York: Harcourt Brace Jovanovich.
Crews, D. 1995. *Sail Away.* New York: Greenwillow Books, William Morrow & Company.
Duke, K. 1984. *Guinea Pigs Far and Near.* New York: E. P. Dutton.
Ginsberg, M. 1985. *Across the Stream.* New York: Viking Penguin Inc.
Hill, E. 1980. *Where's Spot.* New York: Puffin Books.
Hoban, T. 1973. *Over, Under and Through and Other Spatial Concepts.* New York: Macmillan.
Hutchins P. 1968. *Rosie's Walk.* New York: Macmillan.

Mathematics Theme

1. Numbers

Adams, P. 1979. *There Were Ten in a Bed.* New York: Child's Play International.
Allbright, V. 1985. *Ten Go Hopping.* Boston: Faber & Faber.
Boynton, S. 2000. *Hippos Go Berserk!* New York: Little Simon, Simon & Schuster.
Children of La Loche and Friends. 1984. *Byron and His Balloon.* Edmonton, Alberta: Tree Frog Press.
Christelow, E. 1989. *Five Little Monkeys Jumping on the Bed.* New York: Scholastic.
Cutler, E. 1985. *If I Were a Cat I Would Sit in a Tree.* Montreal, Quebec: A Tundra Book.
Hutchins, P. 1986. *The Doorbell Rang.* New York: Greenwillow.
Keats, E. 1971. *Over In The Meadow.* New York: Scholastic Book Services.
Lindberg, R. 1995. *The Midnight Farm.* Puffin Pied Piper Books, The Penguin Group.
Lottridge, C. 1986. *One Watermelon Seed.* Toronto: Oxford University Press.
Magnuson, K. 1998. *A Cake All for Me.* New York: Scholastic.
Mayer, M. 1978. *Little Monster's Counting Book.* Racine, WI: Golden Press, Western Publishing Company.
Pomerantz, C. 1984. *One Duck, Another Duck.* New York: Greenwillow Books, a Division of William Morrow & Company.
Reid, B. 1992. *Two by Two.* Richmond Hill, Ontario: North Winds Press.
Walton, R. 1998. *So Many Bunnies.* New York: Lothrop Lee & Shepard Books, a Division of William Morrow & Company.
———. 2000. *One More Bunny.* New York: Lothrop, Lee & Shepard Books, a Division of William Morrow & Company.
Williams, S. 1998. *Let's Go Visiting.* New York: Harcourt Brace & Company.

2. Time Concepts

Baum, A. & J. Baum. 1973. *One Bright Monday Morning*. New York: Pinwhell Books, Knopf Pantheon.
Carle, E. 1977. *The Grouchy Lady Bug*. New York: Harper Collins.
———. 1987. *The Very Hungry Caterpillar*. New York: Philomel Books.
———. 1993. *Today Is Monday*. New York: Putnam & Grosset Book Group.
Sendak, M. 1962. *Chicken Soup with Rice*. New York: Scholastic.

AUTHOR STUDIES

Paulette Bourgeois Books

Bourgeois, P. 1986. *Franklin in the Dark*. Toronto: Kids Can Press.
———. 1989. *Hurry up Franklin*. Toronto: Kids Can Press.
———. 1991. *Franklin Fibs*. Toronto: Kids Can Press.
———. 1992. *Franklin Is Lost*. Toronto: Kids Can Press.
———. 1993. *Franklin Is Bossy*. Toronto: Kids Can Press.
———. 1994. *Franklin Is Messy*. Toronto: Kids Can Press.
———. 1995. *Franklin and the Tooth Fairy*. Toronto: Kids Can Press.
———. 1995. *Franklin Goes to School*. Toronto: Kids Can Press.
———. 1995. *Franklin Plays the Game*. Toronto: Kids Can Press.
———. 1995. *Franklin Wants a Pet*. Toronto: Kids Can Press.
———. 1995. *Franklin's Blanket*. Toronto: Kids Can Press.
———. 1996. *Franklin Has a Sleep Over*. Toronto: Kids Can Press.
———. 1996. *Franklin's Bad Day*. Toronto: Kids Can Press.
———. 1996. *Franklin's School Play*. Toronto: Kids Can Press.
———. 1997. *Finders Keepers for Franklin*. Toronto: Kids Can Press.
———. 1997. *Franklin Rides a Bike*. Toronto: Kids Can Press.
———. 1997. *Franklin's New Friend*. Toronto: Kids Can Press.
———. 1998. *Franklin and the Thunder Storm*. Toronto: Kids Can Press.
———. 1998. *Franklin's Christmas Gift*. Toronto: Kids Can Press.
———. 1999. *Franklin and the Baby*. Toronto: Kids Can Press.
———. 1999. *Franklin Says Sorry*. Toronto: Kids Can Press.
———. 1999. *Franklin's Neighborhood*. Toronto: Kids Can Press.
———. 2000. *Franklin Goes to the Hospital*. Toronto: Kids Can Press.

Eric Carle Books

Carle, E. 1973. *Have You Seen My Cat?* New York: Philomel Books.
———. 1975. *The Mixed-Up Chameleon*. New York: Harper Collins.
———. 1977. *The Grouchy Ladybug*. New York: Harper Collins.
———. 1985. *The Very Busy Spider*. New York: Scholastic.
———. 1987. *The Very Hungry Caterpillar*. New York: Philomel Books.
———. 1988. *Do You Want to Be My Friend?* New York: Putnam & Grosset Book Group.
———. 1990. *The Very Quiet Cricket*. New York: Putnam & Grosset Book Group.
———. 1993. *Today Is Monday*. New York: Putnam & Grosset Book Group.
———. 1995. *The Very Lonely Firefly*. New York: Philomel Books.

———. 1998. *Hello Red Fox*. New York: Simon & Schuster, Books for Young Readers.

———. 1999. *Rooster's off to See the World*. New York: Aladdin Paperbacks, an Imprint of Simon & Schuster.

———. 1999. *The Very Clumsy Click Beetle*. New York: Philomel Books.

———. 2000. *Does a Kangaroo Have a Mother, Too?* New York: Harper Collins Publishers.

Donald Crews Books

Crews, D. 1978. *Freight Train*. New York: Scholastic.

———. 1982. *Harbor*. New York: Greenwillow Books, William Morrow & Company.

———. 1989. *Flying*. New York: Greenwillow Books, William Morrow & Company.

———. 1995. *Sail Away*. New York: Greenwillow Books, William Morrow & Company.

Mirra Ginsberg Books

Ginsberg, M. 1975. *How the Sun Was Brought Back to The Sky*. New York: Morrow.

———. 1980. *Good Morning Chick*. New York: Scholastic.

———. 1980. *Where Does the Sun Go at Night?* New York: Mulberry Publishing.

———. 1985. *Across the Stream*. New York: Puffin Books, Penguin Books.

———. 1987. *Four Brave Sailors*. New York: Greenwillow.

Eric Hill Books

Hill, E. 1986. *Spot Goes to the Circus*. New York: Puffin Books, Penguin Books.

———. 1990. *Spot Goes to the Farm*. New York: Puffin Books, Penguin Books.

———. 1992. *Spot Goes to the Party*. New York: Putnam's Sons.

———. 1994. *Where's Spot?* New York: Putnam's Sons.

———. 1996. *Spot Visits His Grandparents*. New York: Puffin Books, Penguin Books for Young Readers.

———. 1997. *Spot Bakes a Cake*. New York: Puffin Books, Penguin Books for Young Readers.

———. 1999. *Spot Can Count*. New York: G. P. Putnam's Sons.

Arnold Lobel Books

Lobel, A. 1970. *Frog and Toads Are Friends*. New York: Harper & Row, Publishers.

———. 1972. *Frog and Toad Together*. New York: Scholastic Book Services.

———. 1972. *Mouse Tales*. New York: Harper Collins.

———. 1975. *Owl at Home*. New York: Harper Collins.

———. 1981. *On Market Street*. New York: Scholastic.

———. 1984. *The Rose in My Garden*. New York: Greenwillow Books, William Morrow & Company.

Mercer Mayer Books

Mayer, M. 1969. *Frog Where Are You?* New York: Dial Press.

———. 1974. *Frog Goes to Dinner*. Dial Books for Young Children, a Division of E. P. Dutton.

———. 1975. *Just for You*. Racine, Wisconsin: Western Publishing Company, Inc.

———. 1977. *Just Me and My Dad*. Racine Wisconsin: Western Publishing Company, Inc.

———. 1980. *What Do You Do With a Kangaroo?* New York: Scholastic Inc.

———. 1983. *I Was So Mad*. Racine Wisconsin: Western Publishing Company.

———. 1983. *Just Grandma and Me*. Racine Wisconsin: Western Publishing Company.

———. 1983. *Me Too!* Racine Wisconsin: Western Publishing Company.

———. 1983. *When I Get Bigger*. Racine Wisconsin: Western Publishing Company.

———. 1985. *Just Grandpa and Me*. Racine Wisconsin: Western Publishing Company.

———. 1986. *Just Me and My Baby Sitter*. Racine Wisconsin: Western Publishing Company.

Mayer, M. & Marianna Mayer. 1967. *A Boy a Dog and a Frog*. New York: Dial Press.

Robert Munsch Books

Munsch, R. 1979. *The Dark*. Toronto: Annick Press Ltd.

———. 1982. *Mud Puddle*. Toronto: Annick Press Ltd.

———. 1982. *Murmel, Murmel, Murmel*. Toronto: Annick Press Ltd.

———. 1983. *Angela's Airplane*. Toronto: Annick Press Ltd.

———. 1985. *Thomas' Snowsuit*. Toronto: Annick Press Ltd.

———. 1986. *The Boy in the Drawer*. Toronto: Annick Press Ltd.

———. 1989. *50 Below Zero*. Toronto: Annick Press Ltd.

———. 1989. *Pigs*. Toronto: Annick Press Ltd.

———. 1990. *Good Families Don't*. Toronto: Annick Press Ltd.

———. 1990. *Something Good*. Toronto: Annick Press Ltd.

———. 1991. *Show and Tell*. Toronto: Annick Press Ltd.

———. 1991. *The Fire Station*. Toronto: Annick Press Ltd.

———. 1995. *David's Father*. Toronto: Annick Press Ltd.

———. 1995. *Mortimer*. Toronto: Annick Press Ltd.

———. 1995. *The Dark*. Toronto: Annick Press Ltd.

———. 1995. *Wait and See*. Toronto: Annick Press Ltd.

———. 1995. *Where Is Gah-Ning?* Toronto: Annick Press Ltd.

———. 1996. *A Promise Is a Promise*. Toronto Annick Press Ltd.

———. 1996. *Purple, Green and Yellow*. Toronto: Annick Press Ltd.

———. 1996. *Stephanie's Pony Tail*. Toronto: Annick Press Ltd.

———. 1997. *Alligator Baby*. Toronto: Annick Press Ltd.

———. 1998. *Andrew's Loose Tooth*. Toronto: Scholastic Canada Ltd.

———. 1998. *Get Out of Bed*. Toronto: Scholastic Canada Ltd.

———. 1998. *I Have to Go!* Toronto: Annick Press Ltd.

———. 1999. *The Paper Bag Princess*. Toronto: Annick Press Ltd.

———. 1999. *We Share Everything*. Toronto: Scholastic Canada Ltd.
———. 2000. *Mmmm, Cookies*. Toronto: Scholastic Canada Ltd.

Charlotte Zolotow Books

Zolotow, C. 1958. *Do You Know What I'll Do?* New York: Harper Collins.
———. 1962. *Mr. Rabbit and the Lovely Present*. New York: Harper & Row.
———. 1963. *The Quarreling Book*. New York: Harper & Row.
———. 1965. *Someday*. New York: Harper & Row.
———. 1965. *When I Have a Little Girl*. New York: Harper & Row.
———. 1966. *Big Sister and Little Sister*. New York: Harper & Row.
———. 1967. *When I Have A Little Boy*. New York: Harper Collins.
———. 1969. *The Hating Book*. New York: Harper & Row.
———. 1971. *A Father Like That*. New York: Harper & Row.
———. 1972. *William's Doll*. New York: Harper & Row.
———. 1974. *My Grandson Lew*. New York: Harper & Row.
———. 1975. *The Unfriendly Book*. New York: Harper & Row.
———. 1976. *May I Visit?* New York: Harper & Row.
———. 1980. *Say It!* New York: Greenwillow.
———. 1984. *I Know a Lady*. New York: Greenwillow.
———. 1995. *The Old Dog*. New York: Harper Collins.

PROFESSIONAL REFERENCES

Adams, M. 1990. *Beginning to Read: Thinking and Learning about Print*. Cambridge, MA: MIT Press.
Allen, R. V. and C. Allen. 1982. *Language Experience Activities*. Boston, MA: Houghton-Mifflin.
Avery, C. 1993. *. . . And with a Light Touch*. Portsmouth, NH: Heinemann.
Botrie, M. and P. Wenger. 1992. *Teachers & Parents Together*. Markham, Ontario: Pembroke Publishing.
Brown, H. and B. Cambourne. 1987. *Read and Retell*. Portsmouth, NH: Heinemann.
Butler, A. and J. Turbill. 1990. *Towards a Reading and Writing Classroom*. Rozelle, NSW, Australia: Primary English Teaching Association.
Butler, D. and M. Clay. 1983. *Reading Begins at Home*. Portsmouth, NH: Heinemann.
Calkins, L. , K. Montgomery, and D. Santman. 1998. *A Teacher's Guide to Standardized Testing: Knowledge Is Power*. Portsmouth NH: Heinemann.
Clay, M. 1991. *Becoming Literate: The Construction of Inner Control*. Portsmouth NH: Heinemann.
———. 1993. *An Observation Survey of Early Literacy Achievement*. Portsmouth, NH: Heinemann.
Dewsbury, A. 1994. *Parents as Partners: Helping Your Child's Literacy and Language Development*. Portsmouth, NH: Heinemann.
Duke, N. 1999. "The Scarcity of Informational Reading in First Grade," CIERA Report, Center for the Improvement of Early Reading Instruction. Education Department of Western Australia. 1995. *First Steps Reading Resource Book*. Portsmouth, NH: Heinemann.

Durkin, D. 1966. *Children Who Read Early*. New York: Teachers College Press.

Fisher, B. 1991. *Joyful Learning*. Portsmouth, NH: Heinemann.

———. 1995. *Thinking and Learning Together*. Portsmouth, NH: Heinemann.

Giacobbe, M. and N. Atwell, 1986–88. Workshops for Pennsylvania Department of Education, Harrisburg, PA.

Heald-Taylor, G. 1989. *The Administrator's Guide to Whole Language*. Katonah, NY: Richard C. Owen Publishers.

———. 1987. "How to Use Predictable Books for K–2 Language Arts Instruction." *The Reading Teacher*, **40**, 656–661.

Holdaway, D. 1979. *The Foundations of Literacy*. New York: Scholastic.

Hopkins, H. 1977. *From Talkers to Readers: The Natural Way:* New York: Ashton Scholastic.

Hoyt, L. 1999. *Revisit, Reflect, Retell: Strategies for Improving Reading Comprehension*. Portsmouth, NH: Heinemann.

———. 1999. *Snapshots: Literacy Minilessons Up Close*. Portsmouth, NH: Heinemann.

Huck, C. , S. Hepler and J. Hickman. 1993. *Children's Literature in Elementary School*, 5th ed. New York: Holt, Rinehart and Winston.

Hydrick, J. 1996. *Parent's Guide to Literacy*. Urbana, IL: National Council of Teachers of English.

Jacobson, J. 1999. *How Is My First Grader Doing in School?* New York: Simon & Schuster.

Lipson, E. 1988. *The New York Times Parent's Guide to the Best Books for Children*. New York: Times Books.

McCain, M. and F. Mustard. 1999. *Early Years Study*. Toronto: Publications Ontario.

McGee, L. and G. Tompkins. 1995. "Literature-Based Reading Instruction: What's Guiding the Instruction?" *Language Arts*, **72**, 405–414.

Morrow, L. 1996. *Literacy Centers*. York, ME: Stenhouse.

Norris, D. and J. Boucher, 1980. *Observing Children*. Toronto: The Toronto Board of Education for the City of Toronto.

Opitz, M. 2000. *Rhymes & Reasons*. Portsmouth, NH: Heinemann.

Power, B. 1999. *Parent Power: Energizing Home and School Communication*. Portsmouth, NH: Heinemann.

Routman, R. 1991. *Invitations*. Portsmouth, NH: Heinemann.

———. 2000. *Conversations: Strategies for Teaching, Learning, and Evaluating*. Portsmouth, NH: Heinemann.

Savage, J. 1998. *Teaching Reading and Writing: Combining Skills, Strategies, and Literature*. New York: McGraw-Hill.

Slaughter, J. 1993. *Beyond Story Books: Young Children and the Shared Book Experience*. Newark, DE: International Reading Organization.

Stewig J. 1988. *Children & Literature*. Boston, MA: Houghton-Mifflin.

Teale, W. 1984. "Reading to Young Children: Its Significance for Literacy Development. " In *Awakening to Literacy*, eds. H. Goelman, A. Oberg, and F. Smith. Portsmouth, NH: Heinemann.

Temple, C., M. Martinez, J. Yokota and A. Naylor. 1998. *Children's Books in Children's Hands*. Boston, MA: Allyn and Bacon.

Tompkins, G. 1998. *Language Arts: Content and Teaching Strategies*. Upper Saddle River, NJ: Prentice Hall.

Tunnell, M. and J. Jacobs. 1989. "Using 'Real' Books: Research Findings on Literature-Based Reading Instruction." *The Reading Teacher* **42**(7): 470–477.

International Reading Association and National Council of Teachers of English. 1996. *Standards for the English Language Arts.* Newark, Delaware: International Reading Association, and Urbana, IL: National Council of Teachers of English.

Weaver, C. 1994. *Reading Process and Practice: From Socio-Psycholinguistics to Whole Language.* 2nd ed. Portsmouth, NH: Heinemann.

Wells, G. 1986. *The Meaning Makers: Children Learning Language and Using Language to Learn.* Portsmouth, NH: Heinemann.

Index

....